MARCA -RELLI

MARCA

DANIEL GIRALT- MIRACLE

Preface: HAROLD ROSENBERG

EDICIONES POLIGRAFA, S.A.

MARCA-RELLI

Daniel Giralt-Miracle
Preface: Harold Rosenberg

Ediciones Polígrafa, S. A. - Balmes, 54 - Barcelona-7 (Spain)

Lay-out: JUAN PEDRAGOSA

I. S. B. N. 84-343-0229-2

CONTENTS

so many selves (so many fiends and gods
each greedier than every) is a man
(so easily one in another hides;
yet man can, being all, escape from none)

so huge a tumult is the simplest wish:
so pitiless a massacre the hope
most innocent (so deep's the mind of flesh
and so awake what waking calls asleep)

so never is most lonely man alone
(his briefest breathing lives some planet's year,
his longest life's a heartbeat of some sun;
his least unmotion roams the youngest star)

—how should a fool that calls him "I" presume
to comprehend not numerable whom?

e. e. cummings

I had seen some abstract paintings by Marca-Relli a few years after the war, but the first strong impression made on me by his canvases was a show of his "cityscapes", paintings of dim walls with uneven holes and arches in them, some with perforations as by shrapnel – and all devoid of people. I sensed in these scenes an estranged mood of obsessive intensity, which is no doubt why I remember them. Marca-Relli's empty, brooding piazzas have been compared with de Chirico's. But they are more somber than theatrical, and might just as well be associated with Edward Hopper's deserted streets and bedrooms, though they lack Hopper's nostalgic detail.

Chirico and Hopper – Marca-Relli is both Italian and New England (New York). Or neither one nor the other, but a man who lives between the two. He was born in Massachusetts, grew up as an artist in Greenwich Village, and has been in and out of New York and Rome ever since. Something related to the mood of that punctured architecture builds up in him periodically and prevents him from sitting still. He arrives among artist friends in New York City, on Long Island, in Florida, in Ibiza, buys or builds a house, appears to settle down – then, suddenly, he is gone.

So today Marca-Relli is a two-continent nomad: sports cars, dark glasses, immaculately groomed beard, beach costumes, a pearly smile, beautiful Anita, his South American wife. He is just this side of being *di* Marca-Relli. The identifying quality of both his personality and his art is elegance. But it is a firm elegance, not the mere shine of cosmopolitan fashion. Marca-Relli's manner has its grounding in the peak period of New York art-world styles, when its forms ranged from the rabbinical-cum-British-gentleman intellectual scrupulousness of Barnett Newman, the black Spanish loftiness of Esteban Vicente, to the prim New England austerity of Bradley Tomlin. Beneath Marca-Relli's Via Veneto purr is the heritage of analytical clarity and formal comprehensiveness of the great re-assessment of art achieved by the Eighth Street debate in the decade after the war.

This mental clarity collaborates with, though it extends beyond, Marca-Relli's Italian disposition toward craftsmanship. It is his way of finishing his paintings and collages that differentiates them from the creations of his contemporaries such as Kline, Pollock, de Kooning.

In the early fifties, when Marca-Relli embarked on his pressurized cityscapes, a powerful nucleus of skill, sophistication and theoretical insight had been forming itself in New York art, though few individual artists had yet conceived a distinct idea of where their work was going. Very soon, however, the mainstream of Action painting and expressive abstraction emerged, and Marca-Relli headed into the center of it. He was drawn unerringly to the richest creations of the new American art: the eloquent shapes and evocative contours of de Kooning's white-on-black paintings and his ink-on-cardboard drawings of the late forties and his extraordinary women figures of the fifties.

With his entry into abstraction, Marca-Relli's dark, unpeopled cities gave way to masks and mannikins and dynamic flowings of forms; the blank edifices were replaced by outlines of heads, shoulders, torsos, legs, as well as shapes that evade direct identification. The new images were not, like the architectural subjects, kept under the restraint of natural appearances — the form of a leg or torso could be sliced off at will, shifted into arbitrary relations with other forms, or left open for applications of pigment. In the painting-collage "Seated Figure", 1954, Marca-Relli already demonstrates his mastery in orchestrating these complex possibilities.

Marca-Relli's depth lay in perceiving that for an abstract composition to be emotionally moving, the management of its spatial relations had to be complemented by psychologically affective shapes, neutral areas and textures. It is their content of feeling that connects his late collages, such as M-3-73, S-15-72, and M-1-73, his strap-constructed reliefs and sculptures of 1969, his figures and Action compositions of the mid-fifties with those deserted edifices of the cityscapes.

An innovating approach to collage provided him with the technical means for inlaying significant shapes on the picture surface and suspending them below it, as in a painting by Pollock. In canvas, wood, plexiglas, metal, he tailored separate units of feeling-charged "figure forms" (the title of one of his 1957 collages), which he could juxtapose like parts of a jigsaw puzzle or superimpose one upon the other. While his imagination manifests itself in the shapes and their arrangement, his ingenuity is revealed in the multiple ways he has devised for holding these shapes together. From traditional pasting, he moved to pins and staples, rivets, grummetted straps, machine screws, used, together with painted simulations, to form elements of pattern in his compositions.

The advantages derived by Marca-Relli's art from his technical virtuosity become plain when one compares his creations with those of other artists who translated Action painting forms into solid substances capable of being assembled. Works made of discarded railroad ties or parts of wrecked automobiles soon developed a monotonous effect, to escape which the artists resorted to new factory-produced materials which carried them away from the style that had inspired them.

In contrast, Marca-Relli's expanding repertory of substances and construction devices has enabled him to play variations upon, and continually to enrich, a coherent theme. Through twenty-five years of experiment, his creations have realized means after means for confronting the spectator with images as wilful and enigmatic as those silent, emotion-laden walls of his early days.

Harold Rosenberg

INTRODUCTION

In the work of this American painter of Italian parentage, there is the very important fact that Marca-Relli represents a decisive stage in the passing of the focus of innovation in painting from Europe to America. Neither Paris nor Rome has been the sole centre of avant-garde art since America decided to take a leading role in the fascinating game of working out and launching movements that reflect the varying evolution of the life, taste and civilization of our time. While in the case of the friends of his youth, all of them practitioners of the abstract expressionism of the New York School, we find a distinct urge to break with the whole European context and create something truly original and native —even though many of them are, culturally speaking, products of the Old World— in the case of Marca-Relli the links with Europe are clear, intentional and evident. He looks for revelation to the great European masters, from the Renaissance to Cubism, so as to be able, after a long process of personal toil and mental evolution, to reach a goal that he has always had intuitively before him and has been steadily approaching, especially in his more recent work.

For reasons of character and temperament, this particular member of the New York School —to which he has given so much more than he has received from it— has always held himself rather aloof from the great masters of "dripping" and action painting, because he was seeking something different, was interested in a personal reality that he could not find either in the collectivism of the groups or in the launching of opportunistic trends. Marca-Relli is really what we might call a researcher of painting, which he sees as a kind of mathematical problem. His studio-workshops are authentic laboratories, his working methods almost those of a scientist. He never takes a step in his work without asking himself whether what he is about to do is true or false, whether it really interests him, whether it is valid or not. The different periods in his career do not correspond exactly to a linear evolution, an unwavering forward movement, but they are not backward steps either: what he does is to go right to the bottom of a basic problem that he has first stated to himself, whether it coincides with the trend of the moment (as was the case in the nineteen-fifties) or is, at least apparently, at some remove from the constant ebb and flow of art-world fashion.

It is this essential characteristic of his career as a painter that singles him out most decisively; it is also the one we first discover on coming into contact with the man himself, his arguments and his work. The changes have been various;

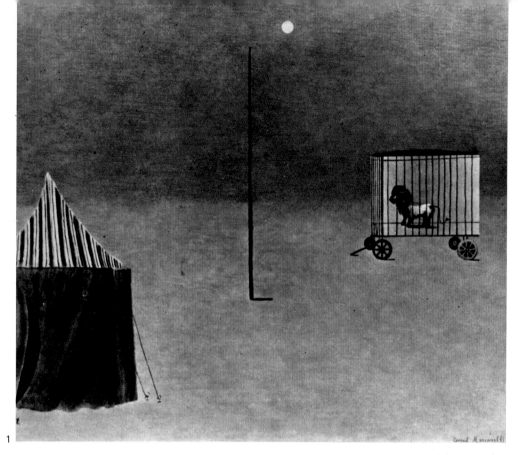

1. Carnival. 1948.

the development, though not radical, evident. But the logic of his work, his method of analysis and the final execution in plastic form are still, in all cases and at all times, unusually scrupulous and conscientious. These, and others that will appear in this book, are the reasons that have made Marca-Relli a painter of considerable repute among the critics but rather less well-known to the majority of art-lovers, for despite his having lived through the gestation and early struggles of the New York School, he has always preferred to go his own way, seeking neither facile popularity nor instant mythification; he feels bound to regard his work as something very serious, too serious for the usual launchings and publicity campaigns. And this is what has enabled him to maintain his moral independence and attain, in his maturity, to the plenitude of a creative *oeuvre* that is unaffected by the ups and downs inherent in the development of "isms".

He has neither sought impassioned controversy nor provoked any radical breaks. His personal seriousness is matched by a solidity of artistic achievement that can only be compared to that of the Renaissance masters he has always revered —and from whom he has learnt so much. In the fields of painting, collage and drawing he has always worked with insistence, with passionate absorption. And from the great mas-

ters he has taken the elements he needed as a starting-point for his journey into a world of research in space.

Form, which is the principal element in all his periods, takes on unexpected outlines, submits to the resolute will of its creator. Angles and curves, closed lines and open spaces, all combine to make up a visual language which has come to be so specific and original that today, in any collective show, any museum, any catalogue, we can distinguish Marca-Relli's "action" or "edges" from those of any other painter of his generation.

In its particular way of treating the masses and the architecture of a picture, his work does not lend itself to any of those types of formalism that gratify the eye or make concessions to the general structure of the whole. In the paintings of Marca-Relli, diversified and polymorphous though they be, nothing is ever superfluous or to seek. He himself admits that to achieve this special balance he has to struggle enormously in the process of definition of each of his works.

Hence his reserved attitude towards those American painters of the nineteen-thirties, forties and fifties who set out to create a movement in plastic art in which the automatic, improvised and direct prevailed. As a phenomenon and a way of practising art, such an original and different discovery in the history of painting was bound to interest Marca-Relli hugely; but his reasoning mind, as much as his instinct as a poet of painting, an architect of forms, has always mistrusted uncontrolled spontaneity. His work represents a kind of search for a divine proportion of his own, for a method of composing masses and spaces in such a way as to leave them interlocked, solidly based and harmoniously constructed. The right angles disappear in the interests of a symbology, half-geometrical, half-emblematic, which becomes the focus of our attention.

In Marca-Relli we find a well-matured synthesis that combines the Mediterranean spirit of harmonious aesthetics with the American feeling for action and pragmatism. Cubist experiments and the lessons of metaphysics are reinforced by the strength of abstract expressionism. Constructive rationality (Cubism), disquieting mystery and fantasy (metaphysical painting) and the imperious freedom and force of colour and form (action painting) are blended together in the painter's work into that half-figurative, half-abstract world in which he so loves to swing — and from which he takes at every turn just what he needs, just what the intrinsic solution of pictorial problems suggests to him. Painting for Marca-Relli, quite apart from any sort of influence, is in itself a privileged and special field of endeavour. Critics and tastes, fashions and promotions, have a habit of spoiling what the painters could achieve if they were left alone to work in peace.

If this rule is not universally applicable, Marca-Relli has at least definitely proved it to be valid for him. By solving the problems of painting in themselves, without any addition or diminishment, he has succeeded in defining an iconographical world in which he is as recognizable as Wassily Kandinsky, Joan Miró or Jackson Pollock.

The economy of means — whether in colour, in form or in gesture — that has always characterized his work is so austere as to be almost frightening, especially when we see it growing more and more simplified, reduced to absolutely essential, schematic values. This progressive reduction to the elemental has the effect of increasing the expressiveness of his forms. Signs, gestures and outlines are all stylized, recovering their original force and revealing themselves in synthesis without ornament or rhetoric, so that they gain greater intensity and visual penetration.

2. Still Life. 1952-1953. Oil and canvas collage
100 × 127 cm. Collection of the artist.

2

The inner life-basis of his painting language lies in his ability to enunciate the problems of the void in such a way as to give it a tangible dimension in space. The method he follows in his paintings and collages is that of using his forms so that they close and open to define spatial areas charged with intensity, in which absence and presence alternate, parley or complete each other in harmonic counterpoint. But while most of the painters of his generation stuck to the highroad of extroversion and devoted their efforts to manifesting man's content of energy through forms, Marca-Relli chose to go in the opposite direction, investigating the possibilities of space in its innermost heart, penetrating by introversion to the abysses of being, of doing, of thinking.

His method is centripetal: he always seeks the nucleus, the very core of the composition, as origin and consequence, as the revolving axis of the outer contours enclosing it.

When he incorporates other elements into his work, however heterogeneous they may be and however ill-defined their perimeters, it is in order to project them towards the centre of the picture, the point on which all forces converge by absorption —and one which he also indicates or draws explicitly in most cases.

I believe, therefore —and this study has confirmed me in my belief— that Marca-Relli is the master of formal articulation; he is an artist who in the field of flat composition has not felt constricted by the two dimensions but has achieved a dimension of infinity, of wealth of form and of volume which we can define as a true entering into possession of space. In space Marca-Relli feels sure of himself, in space he finds himself, in space he is established.

His special contribution to painting has at present the merit of being totally independent. While on the one hand he has attempted to create his own fusion between the work of the constructivists and the questing of abstract painting, on the other he has formulated a language that remains at a distinct distance from any of the contemporary "isms". His figures, masses, anatomical constructions and architectures — whether they are done in paint or in collage — are, above all, works conceived independently of styles and techniques. They are the results of the work of a painter who has always been independent and still remains so, both as a man and as an artist.

CUBISM, METAPHYSICAL PAINTING, ACTION PAINTING

Conrad Marca-Relli, the son of Italian parents, was born in Boston on June 5th, 1913. His childhood was spent partly in Europe and partly in America until he reached the age of thirteen, when his family settled permanently in New York. His Italian origin, the frequent journeys to Europe, his long stays in Rome and Paris, his fluency in his parents' language, and his interest, both theoretical and practical, in the painting of the Quattrocento were characteristics that were to last all his life. Italy has always been his bridge with Europe, whether on account of the language, the aesthetic climate, or the painter's family ties.

His first contact with painting came while he was still at school, where he drew and painted incessantly. Despite his non-academic inclinations and his recalcitrant attitude to the hidebound teaching methods employed there, it was at school that he first discovered his artistic vocation. Marca-Relli says, in fact, that he has been painting for as long as he can remember. But at the age of eighteen he had to take a fresh look at this natural bent of his and decide whether he should carry on with it as a professional or give it up. It was not really a difficult decision, for all he wanted in life was to be a painter and go on working in art. His art training may be described as autodidactic as far as the lack of direct

teaching is concerned, though this was not because of any absence of teachers. He organized his working career himself, visiting museums, galleries, other painters' studios, and trying to keep up with all the events connected with art in New York as well as he knew how. The only formal training he had in drawing was in the very short time he spent at Cooper Union, and this, with a few private lessons in painting and sculpture, was all he had to prepare him for the world of art when, in 1931, he began to work in his first studio.

The influence of his academic training and his interest in the great masters of the Renaissance are reflected in the work he did at this time, but for the first three years he had to live on what he earned for occasional drawings and illustrations in the daily and weekly press. During the Depression years he had to fall back on such assistance as the government granted to artists through the "Federal Art Project" of the Works Progress Administration — a system of grants to painters, musicians, actors, etc.

This project, which had originated in one of President Roosevelt's initiatives as part of his famous New Deal, was of decisive importance to American culture at that time of intellectual despondency. Among other things it provided a stimulus

3. The Port. 1951. Private collection.

4. Ochre Building. 1950. Private collection.

5. Cityscape. 1952. Oil on canvas, 66 × 96 cm. Collection of the artist.

6. The City. 1951. Private collection.

for the group of artists who were later to create that most American of all artistic movements, the New York School. For a painter of that time the Federal programme meant a studio, enough cash to keep body and soul together, a regular supply of materials and the freedom to spend his time on research, without any kind of censorship and without having to please anybody — not even the public or the galleries. Until 1943 many of the painters who were to be the outstanding exponents of abstract expressionism were supported by these grants, which had the further advantage of bringing them into contact with each other, so that they all became better acquainted and soon formed a homogeneous group of artists, aware of their common interests and points of view.

A journey to Mexico in 1940 brought about a profound change in Marca-Relli's work, in all the notions of light, of architectural composition and of constructive simplification in his painting. Both Mexico and the Mediterranean island of Ibiza, where he has had his studio since 1970, are very special worlds for Marca-Relli. The particular circumstances of climate, atmosphere, light and architecture of these two places were to enable him, on this and later occasions, to reflect in tranquillity on his painting, on the *modus operandi* most suitable to each successive stage in his development.

His career as a painter, like so many others, was interrupted by World War II. He served in the army for four years and was demobilized in 1945. Then he took a studio in New York and began working for his first show, which was held at the Niveau Gallery in 1947. This Exhibition and the one that followed it two years later were influenced by the work of two painters he greatly admired at the time: Giorgio de Chirico, in his "metaphysical" works, and the Douanier Rousseau. Marca-Relli's own approach to the Italian countryside or the architecture of the Renaissance reflects something of the sense of hallucination, of the cold magic of mythological scenes, that De Chirico captured between 1913 and 1917, but the younger painter appropriated the melancholy, the enigmatic quality, the haunting mysteriousness of these lonely landscapes with more constructive, poetic intentions. In his earlier works, like *Carnival,* the primitivism and animal themes are given a lyrical touch that brings him close to Rousseau, but in such later paintings as *Roma, Cityscape, The Port* or *Ochre Building* it is the constructive sense that gradually takes over the canvas, the spatial references and the composition of the planes. Marca-Relli himself declares that he was not consciously trying to paint in any metaphysical-geometrical style at the time, but proposing rather to discover the deeper meaning of that kind of

7. Sleeping Figure. 1953-1954. Oil and canvas collage, 132 × 190 cm. The Museum of Modern Art, New York.

7

painting. This whole period is characterized by his approach to the metaphysical "manner" of conceiving colour and forms.

This magic, surrealistic and meticulously-constructed vision of the passing moment was to be a lasting feature of his work. It was this attempt to see in things and forms what lay behind appearances or what they suggested in their very transcendency that really interested Marca-Relli, and it was this, too, that brought him close to Giorgio Morandi in his most delicate, naked and harmonious approach to familiar things and objects. In his *Still Life* he gives us a vision of his subject that goes beyond the "plastic values" Morandi attempted to achieve in such a personal way. He uses his means sparingly, simplifying the planes, taking great pains with the colour-harmonies, constructing with architectural severity and treating the surface of his canvases in a way that heralded his later work in collage. The research he did at this time, alone or with colleagues, received both the kindly influence of the "metaphysicists" and primitives and the rationalizing impact of analytical Cubism. These were the movements which, blended in careful proportions and used in a very personal way, were to influence all Marca-Relli's future work, for in them he found what Goethe called the *tiefsten Grundfesten der Erkenntnis* — the fundamental principles of knowledge, of *his* knowledge. From these influences emerged the Marca-Relli we know, changing his style or his technique, but who always has thoroughly solid foundations to build on. The nostalgic, anecdotal element in his pictures now yielded the leading role to Leonardo's *cosa mentale.*

He now understood why the Cubists had always reproached the Impressionist painters for their exclusive dependence on the *retina* and their consequent neglect of the *brain.* For painting was not simply a matter of recording visual data; it was also necessary to provide for their organization, arrangement and values, in an intellectual synthesis that would discover and select what was most essential. In 1913 Apollinaire himself, in what is now regarded as the manifesto of the whole Cubist movement (*Peintres cubistes,* Paris, 1913), had asserted that "geometry is to the plastic arts what grammar is to the art of writing". And to this revealing principle he added: "Scientists today no longer confine themselves to the three dimensions of Euclidean geometry. And painters have been led, naturally and intuitively, to a concern with those new possibilities of measuring space that are now known... by the term *fourth dimension.*" This dimension, itself engendered by the three already known, represented

8

9

8. Seated Woman. 1953. Oil on paper, 38 × 30 cm. Collection of the artist.

9. Seated Figure Outdoors. 1953. Oil and canvas collage, 50 × 38 cm. Mr. and Mrs. Walter Bareiss Collection.

and incorporated into art the immensity of space, its definition, a certain dimension of the infinite which had not previously concerned artists overmuch. But the Cubists themselves realized that, despite such scientific and psychological content as there might be in their arguments, a subjective element of "mental nature" was also present, one which "balanced mathematical truth". This kind of personal reflection, so eagerly sought by Seurat, was what really interested Marca-Relli; what he was to pursue tenaciously, what was to bring him to that synthesis so peculiar to his work, blending a necessary geometrical order into a subjective, sensitive vision of his pictorial subjects.

The semi-abstract paintings of 1950 and 1951, which were shown at the New Gallery, represent the end of a period animated by colour, still fluid in line and with biomorphic references close to the world of Miró and Gorky, though they also show signs of a tension between automatic informalism and an urge almost like that of Cézanne to construct impressions. Like the great master of Aix, Marca-Relli believes that the creative process is neither scientific nor exclusively abstract. Abstraction begins for him after he has gained a truly profound knowledge of his subject. He studies things (people, objects, gestures or surroundings) scrupulously, in order

to discover their secrets, their truth —not their "realism" or verisimilitude. From this moment on, the picture is for him a result of knowledge and emotions, an encounter between the objectivism of his impressions and the subjectivism of his meditation, his reflection.

The influence on Marca-Relli of Surrealism, metaphysical painting and a certain kind of Cubism was plain to be seen in the show he presented at the Stable Gallery in New York in 1952. Behind the rectilinear structures of the planes, his city squares, buildings and ports conceal an atmosphere of surrealism which becomes particularly evident in the empty spaces, in the light filtering through skies and windows or in the grading of the planes and the placing of the constructions. Soft colours and moulded, carefully-inserted shapes announce the Marca-Relli who seeks a greater reduction of forms and a more precise, more analytical economy of means.

He destroys all the conventional formulas of vision, dispensing with the laws of perspective in order to create a sequence of planes in which the subjects treated, whether classical or modern, will be simply a pretext for the organization of an architecture of space, mysterious and somewhat aloof.

10. Seated Figure. 1953-1954. Oil and canvas collage, 154 × 129 cm. The Art Institute of Chicago. Logan Prize.

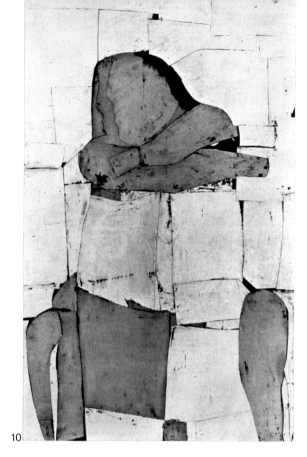

It was in this year, too, that he travelled to Rome again, trying to reflect on his painting in the light of the European experiences and the latest developments in art trends in the Old World. Marca-Relli was to continue to act as a kind of human bridge, for he became a real bearer of tidings from the European painters to America and from the American school back to Europe. He realized that Europe was losing its capacity to launch avant-garde movements, whereas in the studios and workshops of American painters he always found copious documentary material on Matisse, Miró, Giacometti and others. He observed, too, that the American public had developed an interest in things European during the war years, whether on account of increased immigration or because the war had somehow brought the two continents closer to each other. "When I was a young painter," he now says, "we were much more in touch with the latest developments, much better informed than the Europeans, who knew nothing of what was going on in America. I remember, when I was in Rome, I talked a lot to the painters there and found them far from well-informed". It is interesting to recall the words of Jackson Pollock in this connection, as quoted by Henry Geldzahler. In 1944 the master of "dripping" declared: "I accept the fact that the important painting of the last hundred years was done in France. American painters have

generally missed the point of modern painting from beginning to end." But now the young American painters were displaying an eager thirst to learn. Europe was resting on its laurels, looking backwards; it was already exhausted, or at least it seemed to have lost the strength to go on. These young American friends and colleagues of Marca-Relli, however, lived by and for painting, studied painting old and new, talked of nothing but art all day, visited museums, haunted the galleries, studied the great masters, discovered the classics. It was this supreme lesson, the lesson which has always been handed down by art, that was successfully assimilated by the future members of the American School, enabling them to emancipate themselves from their dependence on European leadership.

As is well known, moreover, European artists had a profound influence on the formation of the new American School, especially those artists who had emigrated from Europe on account of the war. The flow of immigration into the States, which had begun during the slump, increased and gradually crystallized into a definite new impetus. The founding of the Museum of Modern Art in New York in 1929, and that of the Museum of Non-Objective Painting —later better known as the Solomon R. Guggenheim Museum — in 1939, meant the beginning of Americans' awareness of their art as it sprang from the rich earth of the great European paintings assimilated and collected. The political radicalism of the nineteen-thirties inspired many of the future members of the New York School to be equally radical in their aesthetic opinions. Another decisive factor was Roosevelt's initiative of the WPA aid projects I have mentioned already, from which Marca-Relli also benefited. Geldzahler tells us that these projects gave the artists a chance to share their problems and their way of looking at life, for thanks to them it was possible to make new friendships and alliances; groups were formed to get together and discuss the most varying subjects, and "schools of thought" sprang up like mushrooms, but hardly lasted much longer. The end of the war was also the end of the WPA projects. Times were hard again, but the artists managed to survive and their contacts were already established. Almost overnight New York became the international centre of the modern movement that was to produce the most outstanding figures in contemporary painting.

THE DISCOVERY OF COLLAGE

On another journey to Mexico, in 1953, Marca-Relli made a discovery that was to transform the whole course of his development as an artist. A technical reason was to be at the origin of a plastic reason. Surrounded by the richly sensuous qualities of the Mexican countryside, confronted once again with a light and a structural system that he had already discovered in 1940, he sought the most suitable medium for expressing the environment in which he found himself, and since pure paint did not satisfy him, he was forced to incorporate materials that were not strictly pictorial into his canvases. He had to look for elements in which the validity, texture or colour could successfully replace oil, or which could cover the surfaces he needed to paint. This handicap turned out to be one of the greatest satisfactions in his life, for he discovered that collage could provide him with the solution he had been seeking for so many years. He had finally solved the problem of how to enrich the visual illusions, how to give greater depth, dimension and values to the ensemble of lines and rhythms that formed the structure of the canvas.

But the collage he used was to differ very greatly — for reasons both of origin and of technical procedure — from the kind the Cubists had first christened as *papier collé.* The basic necessity was probably the same, but the intentions were some-

11. Sierra Madre. 1961. Oil and canvas collage, 182 × 133 cm.

thing quite different. Marca-Relli never tried to pack into a single picture *all* or even any of the elements that could help to enrich the realism of his work. His pictures were never mosaics made up of wood-shavings, sand, sawdust, newsprint or other such objects. Nor did he imitate marble or wood in the authentic *trompe-l'œil* fashion. His was a new interpretation of collage in terms of form and space, a search for new dimensions.

Those strips of cloth or other superimposed elements were not parts of a whole but independent elements in themselves. The painter was not using collage in order to appeal to the feelings, as Apollinaire had wished, nor did he regard it, in Dadaist fashion, as merely a topsy-turvy collection of materials; and he certainly did not consider collage an element of contrast between truth and artifice. While the Cubists thought of this medium as one of the ways of reacting against a certain type of painting, in order later to rediscover the very same technique, in the case of Marca-Relli the incorporation of other elements into his canvas is something like the superimposition of successive ranges of stones in a Cyclopean wall. He simply adds some blocks on top of other blocks. The outlines of each of these blocks trace forms, open and close spaces, create a dialogue between black and white and, behind their abstraction, permit us to make out a kind of articulation in which architecture, landscapes or men are present not as figures but as ideas.

The enrichment of his plastic language in the field of collage was to continue — to such an extent, indeed, that when he included in his canvas materials like the elements of tension in leather, rivets, sacking, etc., their main effect was to hasten the disappearance of oil-painting in his work, giving way to a new vocabulary of textures which proved much more suitable, much more personal. Since 1953, when he first began to work in collage, Marca-Relli has never used it as an isolated element, to reflect or approach reality, or as an element of reference in order to create associations with the outside world and insert them as such in his canvas. Marca-Relli has brought his collage to a point at which it has its own gamut of expression in form and in feeling.

It was William Rubin who said, in 1959, that "...his collages were different because they avoided the textural variation of the Cubists and the associative evocations that the Dadaists and Surrealists gave their work. His surfaces of neutral linen, exactly the same as those of the canvas to which they were stuck, constituted an hermetic system in themselves.

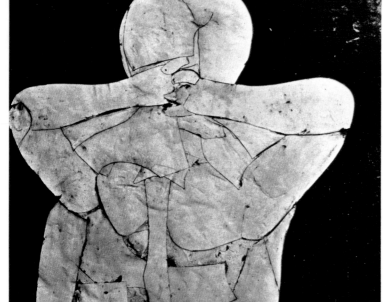

12

12. Torso. 1954. Oil and canvas collage, 86 × 60 cm. Jacques Kaplan Collection, New York.

They successfully frustrated one of the original aims of collage: the reintegration, in more or less abstract form, of elements from the outside world."

Collage enabled Marca-Relli to discover what was to be a key element in his later work: the value of the edges, the possibilities defined by this perimeter of each work, the resources of insertion and composition with spatial elements, with certain very personal forms of his own which he distributes and composes independently of their reference to reality or their strictly iconic value.

If it was to be properly expounded, his work demanded a medium of its own, for in composition he was moving towards a goal that could only be reached with the help of a suitable language.

The interaction of forms, and their successive superimposition, demanded the use of opaque, overlaying, solid elements, which he could never have obtained with oil or with any other type of paint. As for the problem of construction, Marca-Relli had solved it mentally before 1948, but he could not find a way of giving his solution a physical presence until his great Mexican discovery in 1953. He has said himself of

his collage-painting that "it has opened a door I can use, thanks not so much to the material in itself as to the working system possible with it, which lets me think much more clearly, for I can change the forms a thousand times if necessary without waiting for the paint to dry." This constant evolution, this Heraclitean changing of compositions, forms, inserts, lines and handling, enables him to vary each work in the very process of creation until he achieves what he calls the "idea of spontaneity" — an idea which does not appear quite so easily as it sounds, since he has had to struggle very hard to bring about this apparently spontaneous coexistence of forms in space.

In his work, then, collage-painting is a composition based on forms, which takes as its starting-point the previous awareness that these forms are the raw material of his whole artistic production. This "ideology", as the eminent Madrid critic Moreno Galván called it, may not be that of collage as a technique but is at least that of Marca-Relli himself.

Collage was born as an agglutination of content or material, and as an anti-formal juxtaposition; but in the case of Marca-Relli collage once more becomes as much an arrangement of form as any Quattrocento painting could have been for

13. Pink Landscape. 1955. Oil and canvas collage, 66 × 76 cm. Private collection.

13

his Italian forefathers. For him, therefore, collage is at once a problem posed and a problem solved; these forms occupy a void which their presence transforms into space. Although the form may at times be based on itself, it is nearly always merely alluded to, attention being paid to absent spaces as much as to the content-continuity of present forms. But these forms, since they have a strength of their own, a very evident physiological dimension and an explicit spatial urge, dominate the rest —empty spaces, supports in the air, the surrounding atmosphere or climate.

Rather than a pure formal solution, collage to Marca-Relli means a kind of discipline that enables him to juxtapose materials and objects of different texture in order to obtain new results, special qualities and, above all, a particular sort of visual provocation or arousing. "Collage forces you to think and clarify your ideas, with regard to both space and volumes. This discipline obliges me to think in terms of forms, outlines, real and imagined spaces, so as not to fall into the temptation of thinking that nature is a reality." This fleeing from the reality in which he has his origins, this searching for what is a reality in itself so as not to fall into one that is created by convention, is what makes Marca-Relli an abstract painter of what is real.

He begins a collage with the certainty that it is taking him somewhere. He establishes a dialogue between himself, the material and the technique, a dialogue in which a very active "feed-back" determines the final result of the forms. The ambiguity will help to disfigure whatever might seem real to us, so that we shan't run the risk of comparing his figures with any recognizable element. In Marca-Relli collage represents the search, as it were, for a complete plastic language at the objective level.

In support of his idea that painting is determined by the "outlines" and "edges", by these tenuous perimeters which limit or integrate new forms with the help of scissors or fire, Marca-Relli, in his application of a collage that is compositive rather than pictorial, is already moving towards the emblematic gesture that is to be the support of his painting. A gesture that cannot really be called calligraphic, figurative, or violent, although it can be tense; never dishevelled, despite his experiences in abstract expressionism. His handling is always superbly controlled, clearly defined in outline, approaching a pictographical element with a far-off reference of meaning. His painting is gestural only insofar as the gesture is a manifestation of lyrical clarity within his plastic creation in space.

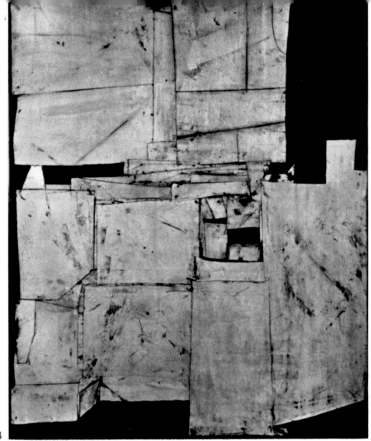

14

14. The Architecture. 1954. Oil and canvas collage, 125 × 105 cm. Mr. Richard Brown Baker Collection, New York.

That is why Marca-Relli may be situated between abstract expressionism (Franz Kline, Jackson Pollock, James Brooks) and the chromatic abstration that followed Mark Rothko or Barnett Newman, as in the work of Louis and Noland.

Among the various generations of abstract expressionists, Marca-Relli belongs chronologically to the first, the one he lived and helped to form. But in his intentions and projects he is the herald of the second, because he was the first to propose pictorial solutions and programmes that were later to be adopted by many abstract painters, once they had got away from the rigidity of gesture or from the unrestrained informalism of dripping.

That is why a technique like collage has been for Marca-Relli not only a pictorial method but also a kind of discipline which, supported by the juxtaposition of different materials and textures, permitted him to obtain strange, more exciting forms. His capacity for rationalization mistrusts — and has always mistrusted — automatisms, improvisations or spontaneous creations of the "all-over painting" variety. "Collage," he says, "forces you to think and to clarify spaces and volumes in your mind; to think in terms of concrete forms and outlines rather than illusory spaces."

Thus Marca-Relli's collage proceeds from certain very personal premises which are based on his working methods and aesthetic convictions. He is not seeking the plastic poetry of Braque or a surprise effect like Picasso; his collage is not the superimposition of remnants stuck together as practised by Schwitters, or of newsprint and music scores in the manner of Juan Gris. He does occasionally make use of newsprint, but his use of this element is never intended to shock, nor does he try to incorporate into his visual world anything alien to the work involved. The role of newsprint in his canvases is that of an element which is plastic in itself and which, thanks to the superimposition of a white background with little black marks, creates a nuanced grey that acts as a middle tone providing greater relief or depth for the flat surfaces he deploys in his plastic architecture. Marca-Relli, therefore, is not just another "collage-painter", in the style of the Cubists and Futurists, nor does he attempt to use any matériaux trouvés in order to recover or re-create a certain type of "picture-object"; his pictorial procedure is rather the result of technical requirements, of personal necessities and of a subjective discovery which is probably useful only to him and valid only in his hands. It is the necessary response, on the material and constructive plane, to conceptual demands with their origins in form.

ORIGINS OF
THE NEW YORK SCHOOL

During the nineteen-forties and the early nineteen-fifties there was a real awareness of, and interest in, painting in New York. Artists in general were passionately attempting to test all the possibilities of new aesthetics. The younger artists made a genuine effort to analyse and understand the great masters of the century. They systematically studied Cubism, Impressionism, Dadaism, Surrealism, etc., though in some part of their consciousness lurked the hope, or perhaps even the suspicion, that America had at least the potential to give a contemporary response to the history of art. Although in those days there was still a certain opposition to such more immediately recent masters as Picasso, Miró and Matisse, the truth is that none of this seditiousness was anything but the defiance of the pupil who, feeling he has imbibed most of his master's knowledge, rebels against him in an effort to surpass him, improve on him or sink him, if he thinks himself sufficiently strong to do it. The importance of the New York School in all its manifestations — and in all its contradictions, for they also exist — was defined in the words of Henry Geldzahler in his presentation of the exhibition *New York Painting and Sculpture, 1940-1970*, at the Metropolitan Museum of New York: "the most recent in a long chain of artistic movements that began with Impressionism and has continued down through Cubism and Surrealism".

The story of the creation of the New York School, during the difficult years of World War II, is a rather complicated one, but it was probably the war itself that gave rise to the circumstances in which the modern movement in Europe succeeded in finding its true climate in this American civilization that was so eager to acquire a movement in art that would be new, American, its very own. These circumstances were further favoured by the fact that the war had forced many of the most famous artists to leave Europe; besides, the little faith that still remained in Paris or London as art centres had been largely lost in the Depression years. But if America extended a warm welcome to this great contingent of European artists driven into exile, neither must we lose sight of the fact that it was these same artists who first discovered, at least intuitively, that the United States provided the most favourable place for continuing their careers; that this young American continent had reached a sufficient degree of maturity to enable them to prolong that chapter in the history of art which they had begun in Europe.

To the already active and well-leavened atmosphere of New York came Léger, Lipchitz, Mondrian, Chagall, Duchamp, Dalí, Max Ernst, André Masson and André Breton, hoping to establish an avant-garde movement in exile. This group

15

of European masters had a profoundly catalytic effect on all the native American painters who came into contact with them — and who were later to be the most vital representatives of action painting and abstract expressionism.

Needless to say, the acceptance of the European artists in the New York art world was not all plain sailing, nor were they everywhere greeted with the same enthusiasm. The weight of realism still lay heavy on the less forward-looking of the artistic circles, and traditional painting had the strongest influence at all social levels. Murals, decorative painting, private collections, art schools, etc. were all still in thrall to the more or less modernized criteria of realism.

These circumstances gave rise to a contrary reaction in many circles. Barbara Rose, in her well-documented history of American art since 1900, reminds us that abstract work was often given the epithet of "vile foreign art"; it was realism, the darling of the majority, that alone had the right to represent authentic all-American media of expression. Joining the abstract movement practically amounted to copying the "degenerate" art (the *entartete Kunst* of the Nazis all over again!) of the Europeans. While the most American style in the history of art was being created in New York, all

the other artistic sectors of the country continued to assert that the true native style was illustrative realism as typified by examples of the "American scene" adorning the homes of a vast public, especially in the murals of Mitchell Siporin, Boardman Robinson, George Biddle and Anton Refregier. It was artists like them, or their pupils, who were commissioned to decorate banks, railway stations, public buildings, post offices, etc., for they exalted the American ideal through a style of painting that was both pleasant and patriotic — if a trifle cloying. But the unerring instinct of the people to whom the Federal Art Project entrusted the WPA (Works Progress Administration) programme of aid to artists, among whom there were administrators like Edward Bruce and Forbes Watson, and art counsellors like Holger Cahill (who was also the chief organizer of the Index of American Design, that wide-ranging record of the history of the decorative arts in America), led them to decide that the traditional art of the time was not necessarily any more American than what was being done on the East Coast; and so their far-reaching programme of assistance for artists, which benefited as many as 3,600 painters and made it possible for 16,000 works of art to be produced in an area of over a thousand American cities, included not only such representatives of easel painting as Stuart Davis, Yasuo Kuniyoski, Marsden Hartley, Jack

15. The Struggle. 1955. Oil and canvas collage, 99 × 185 cm. Mrs. Eleanor Ward Collection, New York.

16. Reclining Figure. 1956. Oil and canvas collage, 63 × 114 cm. Collection of the artist.

Lewine, Hyman Bloom, Loren MacIver, Morris Graves, etc., but also members of the younger generations like De Kooning, Gorky, Pollock, Gottlieb, Reinhardt, Rothko and Guston, among many others.

Even classical mural art benefited from the influence of the Mexican artists Orozco and Siqueiros, who brought to their painting all the power of their revolutionary expressionism. Mural painting in America was no longer to look for guidance to the frescos of the Renaissance, but rather to a style of creation in painting in which protests, allegories, Americanism and injustice were all reflected.

It is for these reasons that the WPA projects have been recognized by everybody — artists, critics and historians alike — as a unique and vital moment in the history of modern American art. They constituted an unrepeatable chapter which influenced a whole decade, stimulated a generation of young avant-garde artists and made possible the birth of the first modern American school.

Although many people still believe that the nineteen-thirties were distinguished by a marked social realism, the most outstanding and interesting work done in American art during the Depression years was in the nature of exploration of modern tendencies, which is as much as to say Cubism, Constructivism, Surrealism, Expressionism, etc., in all their ramifications and derivations. This inclination to the modern in art may already be observed in the paintings done by Arshile Gorky and Willem de Kooning in the thirties, as also in the work created by the group called American Abstract Artists, which was founded in 1935, or even in the works of older artists, especially in those of Stuart Davis, Milton Avery or Alexander Calder, whose style was based on aesthetic values very close to those of Europe or directly derived from them.

As I have indicated elsewhere, however, practically all the historians are in agreement as to the factors which helped to bring this change about at a time when there was neither a market interested in this kind of work nor any public recognition of the contribution that could be made by this new art. The immigration of the Europeans, the WPA projects (which formed part of President Roosevelt's New Deal policy), the creation of the New York Museum of Modern Art and the Solomon R. Guggenheim Museum, as also the foundation of the "Art of this Century" Gallery by Peggy Guggenheim: all these events were forward movements which, in less than

17. St. Cyprian's Day. 1957-1958. Oil and canvas collage, 47 × 114 cm. Mr. and Mrs. William B. Jaffe Rye Collection, New York.

ten years, reaffirmed what all American artists already felt was going to happen.

The end of World War II also meant the end of the WPA projects. Many of the young artists were not yet properly launched, and even less so the trends in art that they represented, but by this time the modern movement had already made substantial progress. Official support was then replaced by a decisive and unexpected impulse on the part of the artists themselves and the society in which they worked. All the men who were to form the vanguard of modern painting had already become acquainted in their workshops or studios and in the Greenwich Village cafeterias. Though they painted in different ways, they knew and appreciated each other's work. Marca-Relli himself, a first-hand witness to all that happened, has told me how in some incomprehensible fashion all of them in a group felt the same enthusiasm and defended the same ideals. In 1949 several members of this vanguard decided to form what they later christened the "Eighth Street Club", which many later came to regard as the true starting-point of abstract expressionism. As all the members knew one another and were at grips with the same problem, they decided to look for a place for informal meetings at which they could discuss exhibitions, exper-

iments and conquests in their art, and invite foreign artists, critics, museum curators and so on to speak. Since individual factors prevailed despite their camaraderie, it was difficult to find a name that would define the intentions and the programme of the group. "We didn't want to create a style," says Marca-Relli, "We only wanted to come up with a name that would define that place. After talking it over for several nights without finding a word or a phrase that would reflect our personalities as individuals and as a group, we finally left it at that ambiguous, ill-defined term of Club." Some of them thought they should have a specific name for the club, "Painter's Club" or something like that, but the others did not agree, for they did not consider that their headquarters should be exclusively devoted to painting, but thought it should be a place where they could talk, exchange ideas and meet other people. Almost immediately appeared the gallery owners, the critics, the museum curators who took an interest in modern painting. Many of them came because they were really interested, others because they were trying to discover new young painters, for since the war they no longer received French painting, which was the real best-seller on the American market. Until some time after the war nobody really saw anything of the importance of American art itself; not one of their visitors would have dared to exhi-

17

bit a Pollock or given more than passing attention to the experiments and exhibitions of the Club, which numbered among its members such outstanding figures as Franz Kline, Jackson Pollock, Willem de Kooning or Marca-Relli himself.

Marca-Relli likes to recall that he was an advocate of the idea of founding what was to be the Eighth Street Club, just after his return from Rome. In Italy he had met different artists who spent much of their time talking about the problems of painting in bars and cafeterias, where they would form the kind of casual club so typical of Latin countries. Some of these gatherings, indeed, thanks to the men attending them and the subjects they discuss, become more famous than the bars or restaurants at which they are held.

To some extent — and as has occurred on so many other occasions in the recent history of art — it may be held that it is from these informal clubs, these meeting-places for artists, that many ideas come which later harden into definite trends. Perhaps the most famous establishment in the more recent history of modern art movements is the Cabaret Voltaire, at No. 1 in Zurich's Spiegelstrasse, where Hugo Ball founded Dadaism on February 5th, 1916, along with Arp, Tzara and Hülsenbeck. That particular meeting-place was later trans-

formed into an art gallery, a theatre and a lecture-hall that witnessed some of the most provocative spectacles of an artistic kind that Europe had ever seen.

The Eighth Street Club was quite as different from the Cabaret Voltaire as it was from the Italian cafés of Marca-Relli's friends, for it neither aspired to become a centre of provocation — though the members did want it to be a meeting-place — nor proposed to make its name as an elegant salon on the Italian model. The Club started with twenty founder members. "We set it up," Marca Relli recalls, "with a lot of second-hand furniture and our modest dues. It was a purely social club, without any pretensions to being a cultural institution or to holding lectures or exhibitions. It was just a meeting-place, where you could spend the time having coffee and talking, for at that time painters hardly ever drank. The most we ever drank in the way of alcohol was beer." After a hard day's work they used to get together to talk for hours about painting and nothing else but painting. To avoid giving the sessions the air of a continuation of work or of a university seminar, after two long hours of arguments they would put on records, have a few drinks and go on talking informally until the early hours of the morning. The whole feeling of the place was one of freedom, of great camaraderie,

18

18. The Picador. 1956. Oil and canvas collage, 119 × 134 cm. Mr. and Mrs. Lee Ault Collection, New York.

where any bickering or envy was confined to the personal level and never touched the member's artistic work. Later on they began to invite their friends to the Club: other artists, critics or museum curators (some of them from Europe), to take part in the debates.

But the time the members of the Club spent on talking did not represent as much as a tenth of the time they devoted to painting. Painting was an obsession for them all, an absolute fever. Sooner or later the results of the activities in the studio of each of these painters had to come out into the light. If an artist on Eighth Street was exploring the artistic possibilities of the figure, on Tenth Street another would be working on geometrical constructions or on forms of colour. They were all struggling for the clarity of a new plastic language. "There was nothing out of the way about two artists of completely opposed tendencies approving each other's work." The atmosphere among them was still very pure; there was no money in art, but no politics or string-pulling either. This period was a comparatively short one; things began to change the moment the group began to make a name for itself. The little galleries started to show an interest in these painters. "An American artist was a new sort of human being." Until then art had always been imported

from Europe, and it seemed almost an act of arrogance for Americans to attempt to paint seriously; but the crisis brought about in Europe as an aftermath of World War II, and the driving force of these young American painters, finally combined to arouse galleries to an interest in this new generation of painters.

The members of the Eighth Street Club never got around to holding any exhibitions in the Club itself, which always remained simply a place where they could get together and talk. The first public manifestation of the members arose out of the idea of holding an exhibition in New York on the lines of the Paris *Salon des Refusés,* since they felt identified with those French painters; like Manet and his friends, all the time they were painting away by themselves no gallery showed the slightest interest in their work, no museum invited them to take part in its exhibitions, no critic paid the least attention to their experiments. So a group of artists, together with Marca-Relli and Franz Kline, hired (for fifty dollars) a place on Ninth Street which was more like a warehouse than anything else, with the sole purpose of holding a show there one day by the whole group. "We cleaned it up and prepared it, all the painters brought their pictures and we held our first show." The more fashionable New York gal-

ABSTRACT EXPRESSIONISM: SCHOOL OR STYLE?

leries watched what was going on with mild curiosity, though they did not hide their interest in those young men who were beginning to be talked of as painters. The very first evening, the opening night so to speak, was an enormous surprise for the members of the Club. Their show was attended not only by the painters and their friends but also by collectors, museum curators and people from high society. It was a stunning success. "The beer and sandwiches were replaced by Scotch and Bourbon, the music we listened to now was 'On the sunny side of the street'." But the triumph of the show on Ninth Street was the beginning of the end. The group gradually broke up and the members became more individualistic; people began to know its members and to distinguish one painter from another, to take an interest in what was going on in the Village, compare artists with one another and understand the new works.

It was then that modern American art began to acquire its identity. For fifteen years, at least, those experiments in painting were still in force, known to some as abstract expressionism, to others as "action painting" and to others as "drip paintings", but in all their different forms they heralded the birth of the first "New York School".

The semantic confusion that plays its part in all painting styles is also to be found in this one. If movements like Impressionism and Cubism were born of the neologisms coined by Leroy and Louis Vauxcelles, respectively, to define them as best they could, half-mockingly, half-descriptively, we must also admit that such terms as "abstract expressionism", invented by Clement Greenberg, or "action painting", used by Harold Rosenberg to describe the work of Jackson Pollock, have not always been regarded as definitive. And still less in the case of Conrad Marca-Relli, who cannot be considered a pure representative of either abstract expressionism or action painting. His work was never muscular or instinctive, his brushwork has seldom been the direct result of an emotional explosion. Although movements in art should be given some sort of specific denomination to help us distinguish them, we cannot strain their content excessively by forcing all the members of a given school into certain strict and precisely-defined co-ordinates. There are many who have hesitated to go on using the terms I have mentioned to classify the "New American Painting" as it was re-christened in Europe years later. One thing we do know is that in the course of the nineteen-fifties all the studios of the artistic Bohemia of New York were set up between Eighth Street and Tenth Street. To say that the New York School is a homoge-

19

19. Pamplona. 1958. Oil and canvas collage, 144.5 × 195.5 cm.

neous movement reveals slight acquaintance with its reality. Willem de Kooning, for instance, was on some occasions an abstract painter, but by far the greater part of his work is dominated by the image of the female nude.

David Smith and Jackson Pollock alternated surrealistic motifs with the purest kind of abstract art. Adolph Gottlieb, too, frequently painted "imaginary landscapes" and even the completely non-objective abstractions of colour produced by Mark Rothko derived, as in a lot of the work of other abstract painters, from an original preoccupation with landscapes featuring surrealistic or phantasmagoric themes.

Before analysing the interaction that exists between Marca-Relli and abstract expressionism, we must really ask ourselves whether it is valid to go on using, in general terms, the label of "abstract expressionism". Not long ago Hilton Kramer asked himself the same question in his column in *The New York Times Magazine:* "Should we continue to use the term 'abstract expressionism' to describe a group of painters whose work quite frequently has nothing abstract about it and, in the last analysis, is not even expressionist in its development?" I believe, as does Kramer, that we should. Although the term may not be a hundred per cent correct, any

more than those of Impressionism or Cubism were, it does serve the same purpose as those terms, now accepted as part of the ordinary language of art criticism, inasmuch as it describes the essential philosophy which characterized the great majority of the members of the movement, a philosophy, moreover, which had a common practical manifestation. Most of the abstract expressionists, according to Greenberg's analysis, made use of free, rapid strokes that were very similar, stains that blended into one another, and instead of clearly-defined forms they painted in broad rhythms, interrupted colours, irregular saturations or densities, textures gone over with a brush, with a knife, with a spatula, with fingers, rags or whatever came to hand. These manifestations —these materializations of the work of art— do partly define the expressionistic element that underlies all the work done at that time. Similarly, the artist seems to feel like an "existential matador" in an "arena" which is the canvas.

His conception of the world is a dramatic one; the philosophers of agony, tragedy and pain are the ones that interest the new school. Hence the synthetic and vigorous character of an art which takes from such previous styles as Cubism or Surrealism the essential elements for transforming painting from a factor of "contemplation" into a medium of "action".

20. Linares. 1958. Oil and canvas collage, 144.5 × 188 cm.

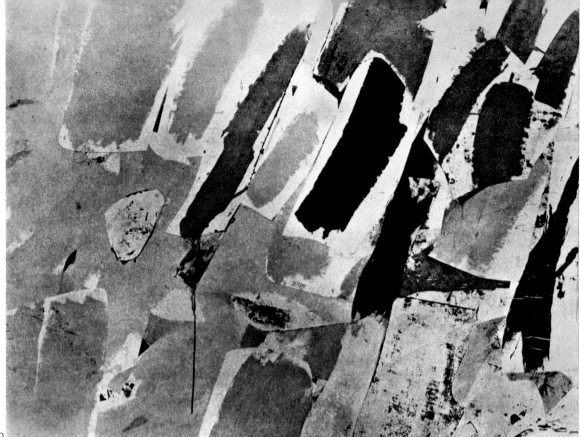

20

As long ago as 1963 H.H. Arnason wrote: "Marca-Relli was, of course, an important member of the New York School in the early nineteen-fifties, but his painting was quite evidently more figurative than abstract, more classical than expressionistic. It is true that there are certain forms of expression and content in his work, but the content is indissolubly linked to an extremely integrated formal structure."

Even when his canvases are invigorated by action, the expressionism of Marca-Relli is moderated by this structural sense hidden behind the forms and the brushwork. He has always liked, and even more so at this moment, to move in what Parker Tyler has called "the fruitful ambiguity", that ambiguity which blends extremes and relates everyday things to one another, and which has a rigid and immovable optic identity with the free, creative force of art. On many occasions, especially in the pages of his "Personal jottings", Marca-Relli has written phrases like the following: "For me ambiguity is a vital force; if I had to define it, I would say that it is somewhere between the two forces of the negative and the positive. It is that area which is almost a hell. It is on one side, but it can be interpreted in two ways. It is vital because it creates a sense of drama, of excitement, by juxtaposing certain unexpected events in painting."

In Marca-Relli the execution of abstract expressionism is disciplined, subjected to a more coherent structure; it is almost an announcement of that phase just previous to pop art represented by Robert Goodnough, Raymond Parker or Al Held, who in the late nineteen-fifties began to give their pictorial surfaces more discreet and more legible configurations. If the years between 1947 and 1953 saw the gradual building-up, in a series of contacts, discussions, conversations and works of art, of what was later to be known as abstract expressionism, it was not until some years later that the culminating works of the period began to be produced, and with them Marca-Relli's most characteristic creations within that movement. Even the deaths of those who were regarded as the visible heads of the "Ninth Street Show" — Pollock was killed in a motor accident in 1956, and Kline died prematurely, at the age of fifty, in 1960 — did not for a moment mean the disappearance of the strength or influence of the movement. Although there are those who still insist on finding precedents for each and every characteristic of action painting in the isolated contributions of pre-war painters in Europe, they are all blended into a single style, a single new trend in painting. It does not matter whether the "action" comes from the *frottage* of the Surrealists, whether "dripping" was already occasionally used by Max Ernst, whether the quick, spontaneous brushwork has its precedent in the automatic technique proclaimed by Breton; it is abstract expressionism that has succeeded in exalting all these techniques and restoring to the work of art the greatest posible freedom in all that is vital and instinctive, as against what is extremely rational.

In Marca-Relli's most ambitious works of that time —*The Warrior* (1956), *The Upheaval* (1956), *Trial* (1956), *The Battle* (1956) and *The Dissenters* (1956)— we can see how the anatomical forms are beginning to fade and turn into textures and contrasts, arising from infinite intersections.

Configuration is present only to the extent to which some parts compose the whole. The furthest he goes in this way is in *The Dweller,* in which the human figure looms up out of an abstract background with superimpositions of strips of slashed canvas in different applications, like a sort of patchwork of free forms. The rhythm predominates over the figure, the basic pictorial element functions apart from the line and the outline. Marca-Relli takes advantage of all the irregularities of the texture and exaggerates them, deepening them with paint in order to give them greater relief. The density of these works is already only a step away from the most ex-

pressionistic of all his periods, the period that begins with works like *Odalisque* (1957), *The Surge* (1958), *Pamplona* (1958), and culminates in *Junction* (1958), *The Conversion* (1958), *Summer Noon* (1958) and *The Joust* (1959). The pictorial rhythm is accelerated, colour mingles with collage and each of them creates forms independently of the other; action enters his pictures. "The great battles of painted forms," as H.H. Arnason called them, are very much in evidence in these works in which Marca-Relli, though this was his most outright abstract expressionist period, occasionally surprises us with works like *Reclining Figure* (1958), in which the human torso is plain to be seen in the midst of the brushstrokes, one or two spontaneous drippings and the formal composition.

We may now wonder, therefore, if at this most abstract, most informal stage in his career, the period of the great stains of colour and the non-rigid geometrical forms, Marca-Relli continued to deal with the human form, even if only in much smaller details, fragments and areas. Are his works of this period interpretations of pores, hairs, wrinkles and gestures, or the piled-up sum of thousands and thousands of beings, out of which he lets separate and distinct entities emerge? However that may be, the action, the agitation and

21. Bar-T Corral. 1958. Oil and canvas collage, 205.5 × 289.5 cm.

22. Junction. 1958. Oil and canvas collage, 142 × 204.5 cm. Whitney Museum of American Art, New York.

23

23. The Feud. 1957. Oil and canvas collage, 132 × 180 cm. Berkeley University.

24. The Battle. 1956. Oil and canvas collage, 178 × 330 cm. The Metropolitan Museum of Art, New York.

the expressionistic energy of the moment are in Marca-Relli and are clearly revealed in the works of these two years that were to prove so fruitful and decisive in his painting, 1958 and 1959. The painting continues to be a challenge, the space of the canvas a provocation to the painter. When everything appears to be announcing a destruction of the analyses of human form and the end of his interpretation of analytical Cubism, when he has succeeded in combining gesture and architecture within a given order, he himself begins to wonder just how valid all of that is. Marca-Relli now broke with many earlier prejudices. He reduced the figurative element, eliminated the pleasant ranges of colour, mainly based on sand-browns and ochres, began to use more exciting shades of red, blue, green and yellow, and incorporated black as an element in the design, as a stain or as drawing. In some cases he worked with blacks and whites only.

Two works mark the climax of this period. The first is *The Battle* (1956), which, inspired in Paolo Uccello's celebrated work *The Rout of San Romano,* updates this Renaissance theme within the conventions of abstract painting. The dialogue between figure and place, between time and space, the role of man in the universe, are all seen by his plastic thought quite apart from any sort of anecdotal or realistic commentary. The selective trimmings of the figurative field go beyond perspective and its strict laws, form is to be found only in the spirit, in the movement, in the impulse of his beings. The various members of the body are probably easy enough to identify, but it is the compositional rather than the anatomical factor that is dominant. It is not a struggle between figures, but rather that of a writhing mass of tremendously fluid forms, united by a dynamic tension. The action of the characters is certainly present; it is not, however, through their state of action and movement in the composition. This is what Marca-Relli himself defined as "the architecture of an event."

The other culminating work may be either *St. Cyprian's Day* (1957-58) or *The Conversion* (1958). In both the dynamic is already action. Without going so far as "all-over" painting, it is true that certain manifestations of "dripping" are to be found here—but in Marca-Relli's own fashion, within a construction and a definite rhythm or hierarchy of orders. Both the areas of paint and those of his collage, based on superimposed canvas, were applied independently. He thus placed the solid reality of certain elements—of collage or painting—in opposition to the visual illusion that might be produced by some of the painted areas.

24

These collage-paintings of the mid-fifties are monumental, disciplined constructions, built out of forms taken from the canvas itself. One of the works which, in their strength and capacity to challenge, place him at the head of the painters of the New York School is *The Feud* (1957). The classical order of composition of the picture is combined with a quest for expressive subjects and for a more spontaneous technique in order to obtain an illusion of unlimited depth and space. In *The Feud* Marca-Relli manages to amalgamate his compositive sense with a formal clarification, so that the expressionist dimension, though abstract and dramatic, is endowed with a strong inner coherence. Black forms that are hard to identify emerge towards front and back with nervous energy, taking their image to a convulsion in which the white of the background, the black and the blue impose order on the chaos. As Nora Selz says, "the tension between collage forms and expressionist brushwork is very carefully balanced," and this balance, so very much his own, maintained inescapably between order and expression, between composition and technique, is what makes his work so original and passionately absorbing.

But in his heart of hearts, as he has later affirmed and as can be deduced from the shortness of this period, Marca-

Relli identifies neither with an abstract expressionism of forms nor with an uncontrolled action of gesture nor with the expressive violence of "dripping". His "tachisme" is one of form and his calligraphy of gigantic signs refers to objective elements. After some years of exhibiting the works he considered most expressionistic without managing to sell them, he always had to take the pictures back, and the return to his studio of those huge canvases "just sickened me to death," because they did not satisfy him. He was certainly regarded as an avant-garde painter, but in that painting he did not see any reflection of his way of being, his way of working, his freedom. All of this brought about a radical change of direction. "I have to do painting that I like," he said. "I have to be able to live with my pictures. It's better for me to paint pictures that I like, so that I can hang them on my own walls if they come back to the studio. I'll have to like their image, their concept; they'll have to satisfy me because they represent me." The decision, once taken, was total; on the one hand he recovered the figure, which he has not ceased to analyse since then, and on the other he was able to go much more deeply into the possibilities of collage and to seek new materials, new ways of adhesion and new forms of composition in planes and space which were to bring him to the very limit: sculpture.

THE HUMAN FIGURE AND ANTHROPOMORPHIC CONSTRUCTION

Almost the whole of Marca-Relli's work consists in searching for a language that will take the human figure or a certain reality as its starting-point and transform it into a sign, to such an extent that it becomes more a sign than a figure or an object. He constantly repeats that he has never practised realism, that his work has never been realistic. However much we may have observed in it of ancient Roman buildings, elements of a still life, human torsos and busts or objects of everyday use, in his pictures these themes have never been reproductions of reality; at most they have belonged to the realm of what he calls "the other reality", which is not that of nature; and which may be very clear in a picture, but not quite so clear in reality. "In a picture by Picasso, for instance, a figure is more real inside the picture than outside the picture." This is what we might call the logic of the artist. "There is a logic in nature, which we feel. And in the same way there is a logic in painting, which frequently escapes us." This is the radically subjective pictorial reality which begins and ends in him and which he brings to our knowledge through his pictures. This logic which fixes no boundaries between what we call figurative and what we call non-objective — "because for me they are one and the same thing" — is what has led him to analyse, over and over again, the enormous possibilities of the human figure. If anatomy has been, more often than not, a rigorous exercise in discipline which has obliged artists to be ever more faithful to a transforming and vital reality, to the extent of depriving it of all the vitality in it in order to create a sort of muscular hyperrealism, Marca-Relli has always been concerned to interpret the human body as gesture, as expression, as movement, as a composition which is transformed through its possibilities of movement and which, in its changing, generates a formal rhythm that may be, in this painter's work, the true "action painting".

His recumbent or seated figures, his form-figures, are works of a true abstract expressionism, one that is loose and fluid, as all human gestures are.

In the human figure he discovers all the possible forms, all the constructions that may interest him, because the human figure creates spaces and determines or delimits its surroundings. He never limits it to a given position —for man, by his very nature, is never static.

"I cannot control the image; it comes into my mind and is there transformed into reality, so I have to change it all and adapt it to my reality: that is why it is not the copy of a figure."

25. Seated Figure. 1966.
    Oil and canvas collage,
    48.5 × 17.5 cm.

26. Figure. 1966. Oil and
    canvas collage, 48.5
    × 38.2 cm.

25

26

The physical positions, and especially all the contorsions, of our bodies are strained, if not by reality at least by the fiction of Marca-Relli. "If you look at the figure of a woman lying in bed, you will realize that her legs, her arms, her head are all moving, and after the movement you no longer remember what their position was before, all you remember is the rhythm — whether it was a soft figure or not, voluminous or not, warm or not." What in one aspect might be regarded as a facility is for Marca-Relli a difficulty. To reflect a movement in the most realistic way, to crystallize a gesture as in a photograph, is an exercise that can be learnt in all the Fine Art academies; but to capture the movement in itself, not as a dynamism of forms in the course of transformation, as the Futurists did, but as a reflection of a kinetism in action, that is a much more complex undertaking. In most of Marca-Relli's abstract pictures reflecting a man or a woman, the sex is never determined. He does not confine himself to presenting a position or an attitude, what we call a "pose"; on the contrary, the infinitesimal displacements of every muscle, the multiple variations of a kneecap or the different flexions of the whole body are reflected to a degree of indeterminateness that is clear enough for us to understand it. "I am still trying to discover what the expression of the figure is. The face, the eyes, the hands, even the strength,

these things reflect only the form, only an imaginary figure, but they are the most real part for me, they are the figure and the image."

While the human compositions in the works of Renaissance artists gave a grandiose vision of spaces, the human beings of Marca-Relli are isolated and independent; at most they are superimposed, overlapping, appearing before us entwined as though in a physical conflict, generally without hands or feet, which are details that would demand an over-meticulous treatment. Frequently, too, they appear in mutilated form, in corporeal fragments that seem to be loose, almost free-floating, but which fit into a structural rhythm and define very precisely the members to which they belong.

Everything is form; the body is transformed into a manageable, ever-changing "macro-form", which can be strained and can escape the limits of the muscles in positions that are inconceivable for the body. "How often I have to vary the position of an arm or lengthen a leg so as to create the anatomy of my picture, not that which can be studied of a human proportion." Sometimes the members are multiplied and form a repertory that is too extensive for us to attribute to a single person; but this is only done in response to a simple

27

constructive idea. If Marca-Relli needs more heads, more shoulders, more arms or more legs, he can fall back on his imagination —or, perhaps, on his reality— to create the figurative ensemble that suits him. "When I finish a picture that I consider figurative, it should be seen in such a way that one is not conscious of what a figure is; one should be aware, rather, of a presence, an emotion, a human meaning, but not of a figure."

The elements of the body permit him to interrelate one figure with another, to achieve that "cohabitation of forms in space" which he inherited from analytical Cubism and which, as a final consequence, he was to work out in the abstract and gestural collages of his latest period. The positive of a bent arm fits in perfectly with the negative of a leg at a right angle. The outlines of hips find their answer in the sinuous curves of a bust. The body is space; its members, integral parts of a great construction.

We cannot point to any precise moment at which Marca-Relli paid particular attention to the figure. It is always present in his work; he takes it up and leaves it down again when it suits him, but it always reappears. From 1953 to 1956 he worked on it in different ways, though always

through the underlying method of collage. Between 1961 and 1969 he mechanized it and made it the subject of new calculations, treating it almost as a doctor treats the various defects of the body to which belts or corrective apparatuses must be applied. Since 1970 gesture has remained isolated, independent, free; it is a pure sign, but it is present.

In the early nineteen-fifties some of his painter colleagues asked him if it was possible to create a new kind of figuration on the basis of the body, now that Matisse or even Picasso had succeeded in representing the body so extraordinarily and at the same time so expressively. "They told me it wasn't possible to do anything else, for everything was already done." But Marca-Relli knew intuitively that there was another concept, another way of treating the figure, a way that was different from those used by Matisse and Picasso; that it was possible to take a different concept as his starting-point, not with the idea of eliminating the others but in order to broaden their interpretations.

From this thought was born, or at least reinforced, his interest in the human figure as a gestural factor, an element of composition, a non-naturalist reality. In this sense there is not only a Cubist vision of the compositive element but also a

PUZZLEMENTS, CONFIGURATIONS AND CONTOURS

surrealistic comprehension of forms. There is an expression-ism which may have informalist leanings, but which is also endowed with a real muscularity and physiology.

Rather than constructing an anatomical or any other kind of theme, Marca-Relli endeavours to "destroy the subject" or the central theme, in order that his own solution may be valid, whether by slowly sacrificing the recognizable forms or by exaggerating the rhythms, the composition or the gesture. The surrounding space is invested with the same importance as the biomorphic elements and forms part of the climate of tension or convulsion of the characters. This climate is the true atmosphere of a battle, of a meeting, of a love scene, of a fight, a solitude or a dissection. The human figure, almost always concealed behind a collage of canvas or pictorially superimposed on it, is the real protagonist of his works however much the many and varied morphological irregu-larities of the canvas may try to hide this from us. In his hands neither the figure nor the landscape exists any longer at the naturalistic level, but only at the level of the emotions.

The latent influence of Cubism, the presence of an organizing system based on geometry, was never to leave Marca-Relli. No matter what stage in his career he has reached, the com-position of the forms and the way in which they are inserted, the determinateness or indeterminateness of the edges, the limits of his stains, whether these be pieces of collage or painted surfaces: all these factors reveal a dimension of analysis that is closely linked to reality, the objective reality that we can all see and, above all, the subjective reality with which he appropriates objects and figures.

When the whole of our painting and sculpture was dominated by post-Cubist geometricalism, there were even some people who said that no painter who had not passed through the purifying filter of Cubism could really be said to be a painter of our time. Cubism may almost be regarded as the architec-ture upon which the whole great edifice of modern painting is based and constructed. To this foundation Surrealism was to add the "flesh", as it were, the appearance and the sym-bolic value, while later modern movements in succession —at least down to abstract art— were to finish clothing it and perfecting it in its outer appearance. When we speak of Cubism with reference to Marca-Relli, we cannot do so in any literal or orthodox sense. We can only do so to the

28

28. September 23. 1959. Oil and canvas collage, 15.2 × 97.7 cm.
Mr. W. Hawkins Ferry Collection, Grosse Point Shores, Michigan.

extent to which his severely organized spatial construction escapes the temptations of realistic naturalism and succeeds in offering us an organized texture of geometrical lines and volumes in the Platonic tradition. For the ancient Greek philosopher was the first to assert that "beauty of form cannot be found in living creatures or paintings, but in straight lines and curves and in the surfaces and solid forms produced as their derivations, with the aid of lathes, rulers and triangles." From this it is a very short step to what Cézanne said twenty-two centuries later about "treating everything in nature through the cylinder, the cone and the sphere." Thus in Cézanne's phrase the dictum of Plato finds its historical and conceptual continuity. Today Cubism is no longer a movement; it is an idea, a philosophy or, better still, a methodology. For Cubism itself existed before the actual Cubist movement; one has only to read Leonardo's treatises on perspective, or the geometric ideas of Luca Pacioli or of any other artist like Dürer, to understand that they had discovered the structural element that lies behind all appearance of form. And so the Cubist idea — as a concept that demands of the artist that he engage in geometrization, structuring and organized plastic development, and that he acquaint himself with the possibilities of insertion as a way of closing volumes — is very obviously present in the work of Marca-Relli.

If analytical Cubism (1910-1912) was more abstract, it was at the same time more firmly constructed and calculated. And it was in this same line of calculation and mathematical regulation of forms that Marca-Relli began to work in 1959. Collage is still present; it is no longer used, however, for a dissection of the human anatomy, or to produce contoured forms with clearly corporal allusions, but to produce a new vision, rather reminiscent of Mondrian, of how to organize pictorial space. From this year on all the violence of action is reduced to the force of what is superimposed and what is constructed. The structural organization is simplified so that the more or less strong colours may begin to take a less important role and obey the laws of the form.

For a period of three years — i.e., 1959-1961 — he abandoned figuration for a new abstract architecture constructed of rectilinear contours, uncalculated right angles, rectangular forms, triangles or T-squares. Black, more often than not circumscribed to the different sheets or tablets of canvas, acts as the axis of the construction and the centre, or foreground, of the composition. But the refinement of Marca-Relli, which never permits anything like the neo-plastic harshness to be found in the works of Mondrian, Albers or Vasarely, is evidenced by certain colours, always in harmony with the whole, which he

29. September 1. 1959. Oil and canvas collage, 182.5 × 182.5 cm.

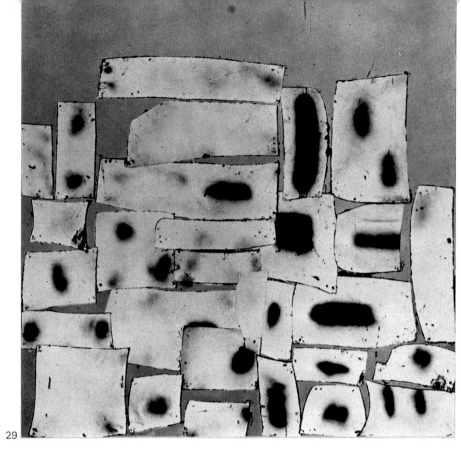

29

places at the edges so that the contrasts will not be so hard. And the various tablets or strips of cloth, even though they are only stuck on, give the impression of having been riveted to the canvas like the steel plates on the hull of a ship. Some are superimposed on others, making a sort of tapestried surface, except that when this is the case Marca-Relli occasionally permits the background colour (red, blue, ochre, siena, green, grey) to appear, in order to give greater sharpness to the foreground. In some works a smoky hue silhouettes the forms even more, as though in an attempt to give them a certain spatial ambiguity, greater volume or an atmosphere of mystery or indeterminateness.

A searching analysis of these works, in which the expressionism and the action are both evident, together with an examination of those which are more rigorously subjected to the rectilinear contours, will enable us to discover a softer, less strict intermediate stage, in which the regularity of the forms is gradually increasing but is not yet taken to its limit. Between 1958 and 1959, just before he stopped giving titles to his works and started putting simply the day on which they had been finished, we find some pictures which reveal the process Marca-Relli's work was undergoing at this time. Each of the abstract brushstrokes becomes more angular,

each stain gradually acquires a profile, the background covers the whole surface of the canvas, until in October of 1959 the first of the dated works make their appearance.

In contrast to the previous stage of formal agitation, this period of the works dated on the day they are finished evidently represents a time of calm, of less striking chromatic contrasts, of forms that are softened despite their more trenchant character and Cyclopean construction. Marca-Relli was now working like an architect, arranging windows, doors, walls, roofs in each of his buildings. In some cases —*November 16, 1959, December 27, 1959,* or even *September 1, 1959* — his works are more like façades of buildings or blueprints for housing developments than simple pictorial constructions. His pictures are fragmentary visions of a skyscraper, close-ups of some great public building, lighted windows in the dark night of a city. They possess something of the architecture of Gropius, or of the building methods of Mies van der Rohe, except that these forms are softer and of a more floating character, with an indeterminate quality typical of the ambiguity that Marca-Relli seeks to imprint on anything that might appear static or hard. The black stains so gently applied have a fluffiness that surrounds each of the pieces in the whole with an ungeometrical nimbus.

30

30. Earth Wall. 1961. Oil and canvas collage, 198 × 299 cm.

The limit arrived at by Marca-Relli in this stage —in which everything was subjected to a process of foliation, so that the layers or scales of the surface covered his canvases like a slate roof or a suit of medieval plate-armour — was reached in 1961, which was the last year of his enthralment to apparent geometricalism. From this moment on the rigour of construction was to retire again to its more passive function, yielding the stage, once more, to a form that is softened, contoured, silhouetted, anatomized. Little by little, as he hinted in some works (which were also beginning to be titled again, as witness *Gun Smoke* or *River Pass*), the angular yielded to the sinuous, the straight line took on a curve, the angle disappeared. The show of his work at Zurich's Charles Lienhard Gallery in 1963 presented the last works done in 1961 with a constructive-geometrical subject-matter. In the later works, which were done in a different way and through other variations, the constant theme was the human figure or the transformation of some elements of such figures into pure signs or abstract gestures. The first piece definitely of this period is a picture already symptomatically entitled *Figura,* which was done in late 1961. This collage, carried out with paint and pieces of cloth, possesses enough anatomical elements for us to discover an evidently anthropomorphic intention, despite its dispersion. The clarity of the immediately previous structures here becomes indeterminateness. From a labyrinth of regular elements he has moved to a complicated jigsaw of irregular forms. The duality between figurative and abstract elements is the essential quality of his work at this time.

The masterly *Sierra Madre* (1961) contains the dialectic tension between that geometrical-angular basis with which he started and the later irregular biomorphic contours also based on the insertion and composition of pieces in collage.

Another work done in the same year, *The Sentinel,* makes the composition still more indeterminate. The colour, too, helps to blur the planes, besides creating a hierarchy of reliefs that give the canvas greater depth. As has been observed by William C. Agee, of the Whitney Museum, *Monk Brown* and *The Passage* are probably the two high points of this period, and in both works the painter employs an evident ambiguity between the landscape, the figurative references and the architecture. These works are the sum of various allusions — which are multiplied and superimposed in a centrifugal movement that makes them cohere — and lines of expansion that delimit them. A floating atmospheric luminosity is achieved by means of the colour applied with a spraygun. Some darker tones of brown, green and their variants are the predominant colours of these pictures. Marca-Relli continues to rivet the pieces of his collages, continues to place them against a dark background and continues to construct them in a double perspective—that of sculpture, which did not take long to appear, and the iconic perspective, which crept in more gradually.

Marca-Relli is a constructor in the most literal sense of the term; his whole work has construction as its starting-point. With his repertory of independent pieces and his range of colours, he first feels his way towards the structure of each work, using pins to hold up the forms he has cut out. He raises them, lowers them, groups them, separates them, gives them a lighter or a darker tone, until he hits on the final rhythm that satisfies him as being the exact, properly-proportioned one that he wants.

And it is precisely in this field of elaborately-wrought creations that he has been followed by the greatest number of imitators. He has succeeded in inspiring a school by personalizing certain solutions which, however varied they may be, however many the modifications added to them, always bear the definitive, indelible stamp of their creator.

FROM PLANE TO SPACE

As a pure working formula, just another pictorial medium, the natural expression of Marca-Relli's painting, collage was now becoming too manageable, it lay too readily within his range as an artist, hardly presenting any new problems at all. Marca-Relli now cut, trimmed, drilled, stained, coloured or burned his surfaces, in a process that was by now very much his own. A process that was partly an entertainment in the manner of Johan Huizinga, partly a logico-linguistic diversion after the fashion of Ludwig Wittgenstein.

His forms are now a simple concatenation of propositions, situated by him in a determined structure which he has previously manipulated and endowed with a greater or lesser degree of symbolism. It was Wittgenstein himself who, in his *Tractatus,* compared linguistic expression to geometric projection: a geometric figure can be projected in many different ways, and each of these corresponds to a different language. In his works there is a logical structure, a determined number of propositions which he solves by means of a limited number of constructive applications. This is what leads him to seek a definition of form that will be broader and richer in expression, one through which he can continue his work and his shaping of reality, so as to be able to work thus

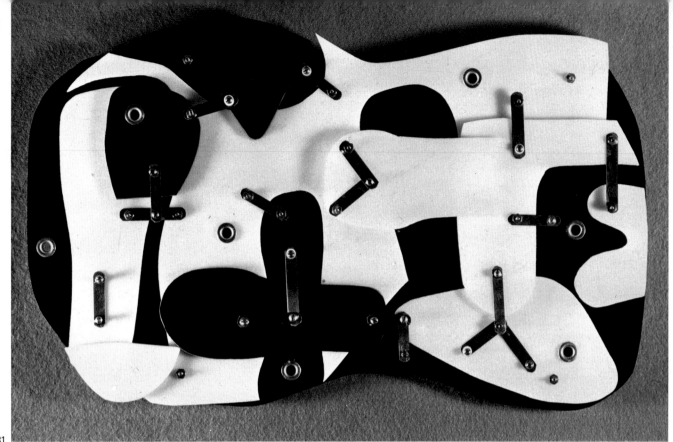

31

31. Untitled Relief 8. 1969. Plexiglass and wood, 58.5 × 38 cm.

in what the Viennese philosopher defined as "what cannot be said but only shown".

The same impulse that had led him to collage some years earlier was now reborn with new materials: aluminium and sheets of vinyl. The hardness of form and construction of the collages done in the three-year period 1959-1960-1961 now reappeared, probably more on account of the difficulty of manipulating the sheeting than from any desire to give a rigid structure to the space of the picture. Few of his works were to be quite so angular as *Cristóbal* (1962); the others were to take an architectural form of metaphysical grandeur and then break it up into large fragments and present it to us in parts held together by rivets. Here the riveting is the real thing. The rivets are not just points painted in oils, nor do they form a discontinuous line of purely apparent or formal little black dots. No, they are an integral part of the process of construction, reliefs and screws with visible heads that help to define and delimit edges which in previous works, done in another manner, had to be dealt with in paint. The initial discovery of the possibilities of the new material becomes evident in the rather clumsy use made of aluminium sheets and rivets in this first stage of the new period. But one year later, in 1962, he discovered in another new ma-

terial —vinyl plastic— the exact combination of strength and flexibility that he was looking for in a flat surface. *Plan B* (1962) is a collage done in this material, with more abstract than figurative forms, in which the ductility of the plastic nailed directly onto the wood enables the artist to produce bulges, wrinkles and edges in relief which determine the different planes of the surface, even when that surface is a monochrome. Everything is simpler, all complexity reduced; the interplay of horizontal and vertical pieces may seem somewhat reminiscent of the 1959/1961 period, but the intention of the forms, in such works as *Runway* (1963) or *XK-120* (1963), is nearer to that of the first paintings done in Italy, or of his 1955 landscapes, than to that pure geometrical abstraction, from which he takes only a working method, not a formal subject-matter.

The vinyl in different colours, together with the volumes formed by the thickness of the material and the superimpositions, creates irregular, eccentric rhythms, deliberately clumsy in their limits but carefully calculated in the ensemble, which increasingly demand relief. Where vinyl is warm, rugged and tactile, aluminium is elegant, rigid and elevated. The qualities of the mineral against those of the plastic enable him to create two very different types of collage, despite the

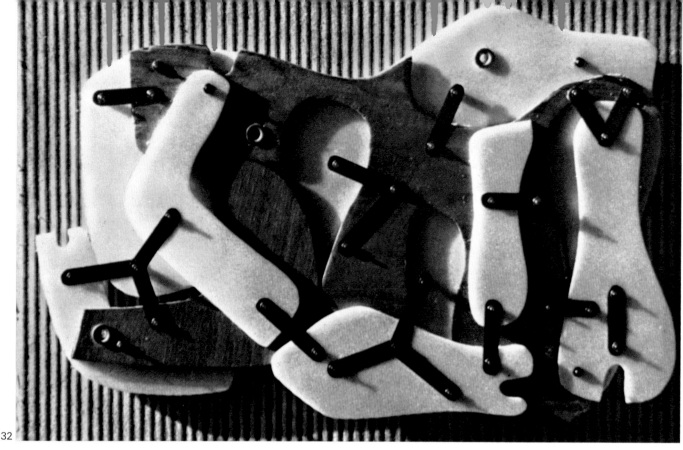

32. Untitled Relief 3. 1969. Plexiglass and wood, 39 × 59 cm.

32

fact that they may seem very similar in his constructive solutions. Each of these forms, if not figurative, is at least highly insinuating. The work I have just mentioned, *Runway*, does not only allude to a plastic gesture very much in the style of abstract expressionism, but refers quite evidently to the fuselage of an aeroplane; but this fuselage is seen in a painterly way, as a form in memory, a mental snapshot, with all the ambiguity or indeterminateness that such an image may possess.

The next step was to be a real leap forward. Marca-Relli now began to like working in metal, to take a sensuous pleasure in its feel, its stiffness, its coherence, to enjoy handling it. The corporeal strength of the metal mass was favourable to his forms, which in themselves were compact enough. Thus formal strength blends with material strength to produce certain plastic signs of open and indeterminate significance but emblematic in their lines and composition. Throughout 1964, 1965 and 1966 sculpture took the leading role in his work. At this time, indeed, Marca-Relli almost forgot that he was a painter. Sculpture took up all his time, but he found no cause for anxiety in this, for since his first attempts in the field of collage the frontiers had already been thrown down.

The question of whether oil paint is used in a work or not, whether the surface is canvas or aluminium, whether forms are delimited by rivets or by burning, does not worry Marca-Relli in the least. Sculture is simply a leap into the space that has arisen out of his collages.

The three-dimensional quality of collage moved from the plane into space, but in much more rounded forms and materials. The ensemble of pieces and reliefs in aluminium that he did throughout 1964, also untitled, took from the old works a fragment of collage and enlarged it to gigantic size. These pieces now needed joining elements in space, and these he placed very ingeniously. Most of these works are contained within oval outer limits, with a slight tendency to squareness. In the inner part of the canvas an irregular die or groove separates the different pieces. Some of these joints even work, so that the pieces can be moved or dismounted. In 1966 the sculptural period began to reveal, in a very special way, Marca-Relli's proposal to bring into sculpture the forms of geometrical collage that he had used in 1960 and 1961. Compact forms and massive blocks were fitted into one another, always by means of an angular or straight-line assembly system. Masses, ingots and blocks close each other up to give the works greater solidity and firmness.

FROM "FIGURATIVE CONSTRUCTION" TO "ANATOMICAL CONSTRUCTION"

The continuation of the sculptural line must be sought in the torsos and sculptures of 1969. These were no longer angular, metallic or geometry-inspired. In 1968 Marca-Relli's constant impatience to get on led him to interpret the human figure once more; in his own style and way of looking at things, and with the plastic strength of the body as the predominant element.

Although his production in sculpture is apparently so slight —though it is a medium he has never abandoned— we may say that his total *oeuvre* shows an evident vocation for sculpture. His work is space, it is moving towards space, it is in space that it best defines itself and finds the essential roundness that gives a meaning to the forms and volumes which go to make up Marca-Relli's vocabulary. Starting from a plane — paper, sacking, burlap, linoleum, plastic or aluminium sheeting— he manages to sectorize this plane by means of some short initial strokes and then adds to it, later, another superimposed plane or a more considerable volume, until the work has in fact become sculpture. But the plane is still there as his starting-point, as the conceptual origin of the work. And that is why we can assert that the plane, even in sculpture, holds a kind of contrapuntal dialogue with three-dimensional space.

And so Marca-Relli decided to return, as on so many occasions in the past, to his constant source of visual fascination: the human figure. His occasional desertion of the figurative in order to work out a simplified abstraction always alternates with a direct return to the treatment of anatomy. A series of small collage-drawings, carried out in 1967 and 1968, now brought him back to the study of the seated figure, to construction with corporeal elements and to the anatomical dissection of all the members which have the greatest mobility or capacity of movement in the human body. In the work done in 1969 Marca-Relli also returned to colour, a colour which was no longer a mere stain but the background or part of a whole. There was also a reappearance of the mutilated fragments of the body; no longer, however, floating in piled-up and superimposed dispersion, but in a new kind of order. The corporal mass is compact now and usually has a central element which pulls it together. The different parts or pieces, inserted into curved forms according to the various morphologies of our hips or breasts, are provided with elements of tension which, like bridles, belts or orthopedic supports, give them consistency. It is not the bony kneecaps or the muscles that allow them to move freely to right and to left; the cohesion of his recumbent figures, form-figures, dual figures, composite figures, anatomical constructions, etc. does not

33. Figurative construction. 1969. Mixed media collage on canvas, 135 × 213.5 cm.

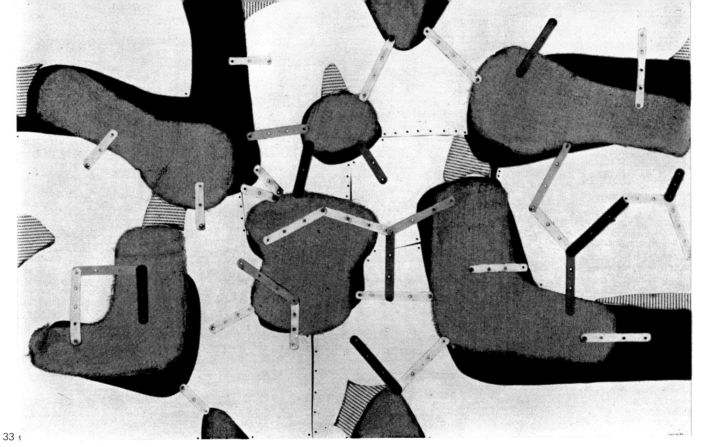

33 t

come from the interlocking of certain contours with others, of positives placed in response to negatives, but from the reinforcement provided by those supports of canvas or metal which are so reminiscent of false limbs or crutches.

It is almost as though Marca-Relli were attempting to pin down the movement of the human body once and for all, to paralyse that flashing bodily movement that he had already presented to us in the 1953-1956 period. Marca-Relli has never wished to create automatons or robots.

Marca-Relli, as a painter and artist of gesture before gesture became a pure abstract stain, needed living organisms if he was to represent what is most dynamic in our existence: movement. With these linear straps and supports nailed in and well-riveted, the painter places on his bodies —or on his representations of the body— a sort of nervous system which transmits to each and every isolated member a centrifugal stimulus that acts as motor or driving force in the complicated mechanism of the anatomy. It is a nervous system which creates closed and open circuits to transmit a living strength to the beings in it. As a plastic value, these ligaments, so to speak, create a rich interplay of textures, much livelier than in his earlier periods. The roughness of sacking on

paper, the softness of unbleached linen on corrugated cardboard, the antagonism of a piece of newsprint on a printed fabric, etc., find in these linking elements a different texture, quality and colour, a fundamental contribution to making them more completely specified and finished at the formal level.

But here once again we can find the latent presence of Cubism as we have already defined it. That urge to arrange, always present in his work, which structures and unifies. This task is performed here by black. Black as a stain, as an outline, as a limit, sometimes as a background. Its presence is not total but occasional, and its predominance is only partial in the ensemble of elements that go to make up the whole. The black in these works designs, outlines and delimits. It probably plays the most pictorial role in all his compositions, since they are frequently done with paint. Marca-Relli obtains this quality of black on unbleached linen or on a surface of sacking both with paint and with the flames of the fire he uses.

It is thanks to the vacillation of the flame, which in its fragility and movement achieves an irregular drawing of imprecise edges, smoky and delicately graded in colour, in a soft

34

range of tones that go from the original beige of the linen to brown, and from dark brown to charred black, that he is able to obtain that admired indeterminateness of the burnt edges. These edges, outlined by his skilful hand, are part of his calculated "puzzlement" of anatomical forms; in the vigour of the black strokes he finds the nucleus of his expression and the most vigorous component among all the pieces that come into play in his abstract figurations of the human body.

From anatomical construction Marca-Relli went on to an indeterminate figurative construction, in which both men and things, especially objects of everyday use, could appear. When he finally returned to anatomical construction it was to see it after another fashion, to construct it in a way that was more emblematic and less corporeal, more idealized and less figurative or realistic. He was acting rather as a true idealist philosopher than as a positivist thinker. For him the consciousness of oneself —the whole activity of feeling, thinking and living— is much more important than simply representing. Without it none of these concepts would have any meaning. He is a thinker who bases everything on the science of facts, not in any physical or mechanical perspective but from the angle of the *experience* these facts make possible in his spirit.

In this aspect Marca-Relli agrees with Parmenides, who held that from the moment one thinks of an object, the object exists.

The merit of this fidelity of Marca-Relli's to the anthropomorphic, whether as a figurative approach or as an abstract anatomical elaboration, lies in the fact that he succeeds in proving to us that the human figure is still a permanent source of artistic fascination and attraction.

When man first learned to draw, what he first drew was man. Between rudimentary palaeolithic drawing and the measured classicism of the Greeks lie many centuries, many doubts, much manual and mental training, but latent in them all is the desire to give life to a human being through graphic creation. Marca-Relli, who pioneered abstract expressionism with his New York friends, worked in the most informalist of all schools, the one which apparently eliminated all reference to the figure from pictures, but he, alone among them all, had to return sooner or later, inescapably drawn back to his origins, his pictorial *leit-motiv:* the human body.

FROM PHYSICAL
FORM TO SIGN FORM

The insistent working-out of edges, perimeters, limits of figures and objects, the deliberate indulgence and the close observation of everything that may represent one end of a given surface: all these have caused Marca-Relli to study, particularly in recent years, the importance of the contours, the different ways in which positive and negative can interlock and the formal equivalence, balance and complementariness of all those heterogeneous elements which, whether by virtue of their very materiality (sacking, paper, vinyl, linoleum, metal, etc.) or on account of their physical complexity, take some part in the construction of his canvases. Each of these constructions is possessed by a dynamic of forms which gives rhythm to the whole play of possible compositions. If the idea of corporal gesture is remotely present, on some occasions this force is contained in an angle, in a limit, in the edge of some stains or in the geometrical centre of his pictures.

The rhythm of his works has an axis: it revolves around a point of maximum visual attraction — generally black, or delimited by black — which centres his whole composition. It is not any kind of golden number or ideal proportion balancing or cleverly harmonizing his pictures; nor can we discover a given pattern that applies to all his canvases. Each of them represents a distinctive way of facing the problem of construction, an emphasis of its own on forms or ideas.

Both in the case of the seated figures and in that of the reclining ones, the rhythmical value of the composition reveals a predominant gesture which gradually assumes the importance of a sign. The constructive emphasis of some of his torsos, or the layered composition of some sculptures, also helps us to find, in the parts or the whole, this eagerness to create significance. The period closest to abstract expressionism is something like a constant superimposition of emblematic elements which mingle in a rather *tachiste* fashion to create certain compositive results. The ultimate consequence of this endeavour to schematize, which has been almost permanently present throughout his career, is to be found in the sign-forms, which have presided over his pictures since 1966.

Figures, objects and architecture, human beings and the most fanciful outline of existence, are synthesized in the essential gesture of certain forms. Marca-Relli does not need the whole corporeal anecdote, the whole building, the complete silhouette that outlines an object, for in a sign he crystallizes the cosmic nucleus, the very core of being,

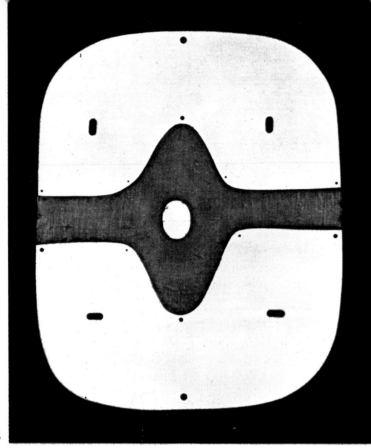

35

the key point from which all movement flows. Trying to codify each and every one of these signs is a complex task, and one that is equivalent to penetrating to the painter's ultimate subconscious. His own explanations, always full of anecdote and imaginative vitality, are of some help in elucidating the intention of these works. When he speaks of a cup of coffee, he insists that the whole mass of china is of little importance for him, since the whole visual force of that object is centred in the curving handle which delivers itself at each end to the bowl holding the liquid. A formal and semiological analysis of the cup would confirm that what really differentiates it from any other container of liquids is the handle, for it is the handle which, at the rhythmical level, possesses the greatest force and aggressiveness. The handle breaks the monotony of the ceramic block to give the containing cylinder an exaggerated, deforming protuberance, which at the functional level will also allow us to establish direct contact with it.

If to the emblematic value (curved handle joined at each end to a cylinder, with free space to admit the fingers) we add the functional value (the point at which we come into direct contact with the object), we shall realize that very probably the rest of the cup is of no importance at the level of visual perception; or not, at least, at the first moment, the moment when we memorize an object or synthesize its form. The handle is rather like the edge of the cup, "for the edge of the form is the point at which a central volume is surrounded by an outer volume; the edge is where this meeting takes place."

To this visual philosophy we must add a decided endeavour to simplify. The work of Marca-Relli is dominated by that ancient law which was upheld quite as much by the Greek philosophers as it is by the rationalist architects: "less is more." The search for the essential, the attempt to pin down the original substance of form or gesture, have made this painter submit his whole work to a process of elimination. "I reduce more and more, sometimes I have to begin all over again, for after having reduced so much I reach such a point of simplification that there is no longer any communication."

Simplification in his case does not mean elementalization, loss of formal richness, or boredom. In Marca-Relli the process of simplification is equivalent to seeking the forms in their most absolute nakedness, without any shows or shams. Taking away the ornamental in order to leave only the essen-

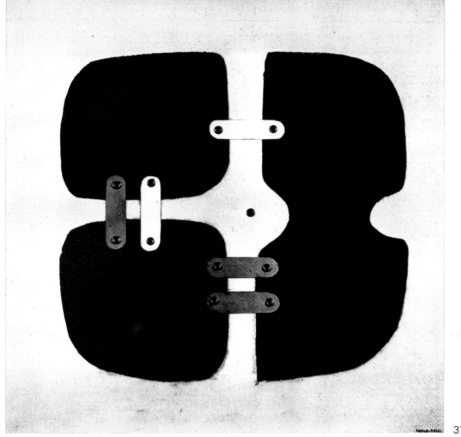

36

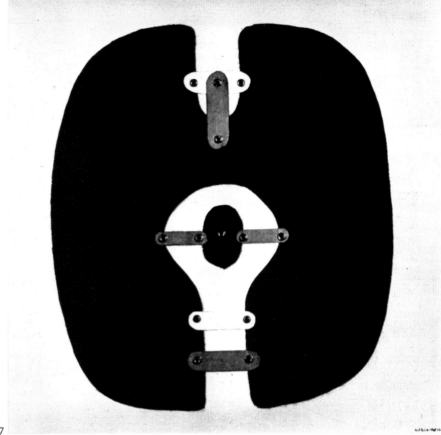

37

tial. He eliminates the superfluous to the highest possible degree of reduction, so as to reach the limit of what is intelligible to us at sign level and communication level. Occasionally he himself escapes; he purifies to such an extent that he finds himself obliged to complicate the form and add some element to make up for the work's excessive nudity. Collage is also the suitable medium for him, since it is a technique that lets him cut out, stick on, or superimpose any fragment of form that will enrich an ensemble grown excessively poor. This simplication by reduction, reaching the essential core of a form in order to discover its emblematic value, its symbolic iconography, is what shows us the most profound, most authentic and most representative Marca-Relli.

Marca-Relli was to continue to call them "figurative works", since they were works which in his subconscious, in the most recondite corner of his retina, had been taken from reality.

But all his possible figurative evidence is in his "visual thinking". His images are in his memory and he uses them to identify, interpret or corroborate something in the field of perception. As Rudolf Arnheim tells us in his *Visual Thinking*

(1969), "there is no clear boundary separating a purely perceptual image —if such a thing exists— from an image completed by memory or not perceived at all but altogether formed of remainders of memory." These remains of a visual experience which may stay in our eyes are what Marca-Relli paints for us. Not the whole form, not the whole reality, not all the representations with all their details. Marca-Relli does not portray; he has never copied reality and he flies from photography. He simply captures some given quality —form, colour, movement— of the objects or activities of man, in order to give us a synthetic representation, which may prove abstract for some but is at bottom the crystallization of the dynamic configurations he observes and analyses. In this regard he follows that dictate so often repeated by the Spanish philosopher Ortega y Gasset: "one should think with one's eyes."

Considering the methodology followed by Marca-Relli throughout his career, it was to some extent foreseeable that he would arrive at some such semantic reduction. Concepts are transformed into signs and signs into symbolic gestures, in a calligraphy that seeks the essential as if it were the distillation of something very complex. By this road he comes to the very fountainhead of writing: the ideogram. The

38. The Brake. 1966. Painted canvas collage, 157.4 × 154.4 cm.
39. Untitled. 1964. Aluminium relief, 121 × 116 cm.
40. Untitled. 1967. Painted canvas collage, 81 × 91 cm.
41. Untitled. 1967. Painted canvas collage, 177.5 × 144.5 cm.

synthesis sign that defines concepts. The phrase that expresses a long succession of facts and events in a single pure graphic abstraction. The relationship between a few black lines, the careful composition of some bars, the close consistency of this abstract graphic world, all of these refer us to the identification of an alphabet truly proper to Marca-Relli. If it exists, we might well ask ourselves whether he has come to it through his need to communicate or whether, on the contrary, this is the result of a long, laborious task carried out over forty years.

As is the case with many other members of his generation, particularly all those who have to some extent been active practitioners of abstract art, the *signs,* the *forms,* the *emblems,* whether their creator understands them or not in their precise or approximate connotations, do not attempt to convey to the viewer anything determinate, or anything that might be conceptually or symbolically determinable. All the emblematic value one wishes to find in them must be sought in the forgotten images of the past of mankind and the individual. This past reappears in every culture and civilization, in the West or in the East, in the most advanced cultures and in the most underdeveloped. It is always connected with the earliest origin of things and forms, which

has led many thinkers to believe in the existence, or at least to suppose the probability, of a subconscious that is immanent in all men, a phase previous to the conscious stage, a philogenetic and ontogenetic "before" which we know as archetypal forms or *Urformen,* the *Urformen* being seen as primitive formal elements which nourish all the artistic experience of past and present, and to which the world resorts in successive formulations of symbols. Both ancient and contemporary works of art take from the symbolic material of the human conscious or unconscious a repertory of signs and forms to which we always, involuntarily, return. Signs and symbols that are quite spontaneous, signs and symbols with constant and almost invariable patterns, but which can be resolved in very different ways depending on the subjectiveness and imaginative richness of each individual. Each of these signs can range from the simplest "force" line to the most centrifugal "circle", from the penetrating "triangle" to embryonic forms, from uterine penetrations to phallic forms, from positive to negative, from black to white. A long dialogue and one which Kandinsky attempted to spiritualize, but which was already spiritual in itself.

There is no need to fall back on Freud or Jung to justify the existence of these patterns in all artistic composition, but

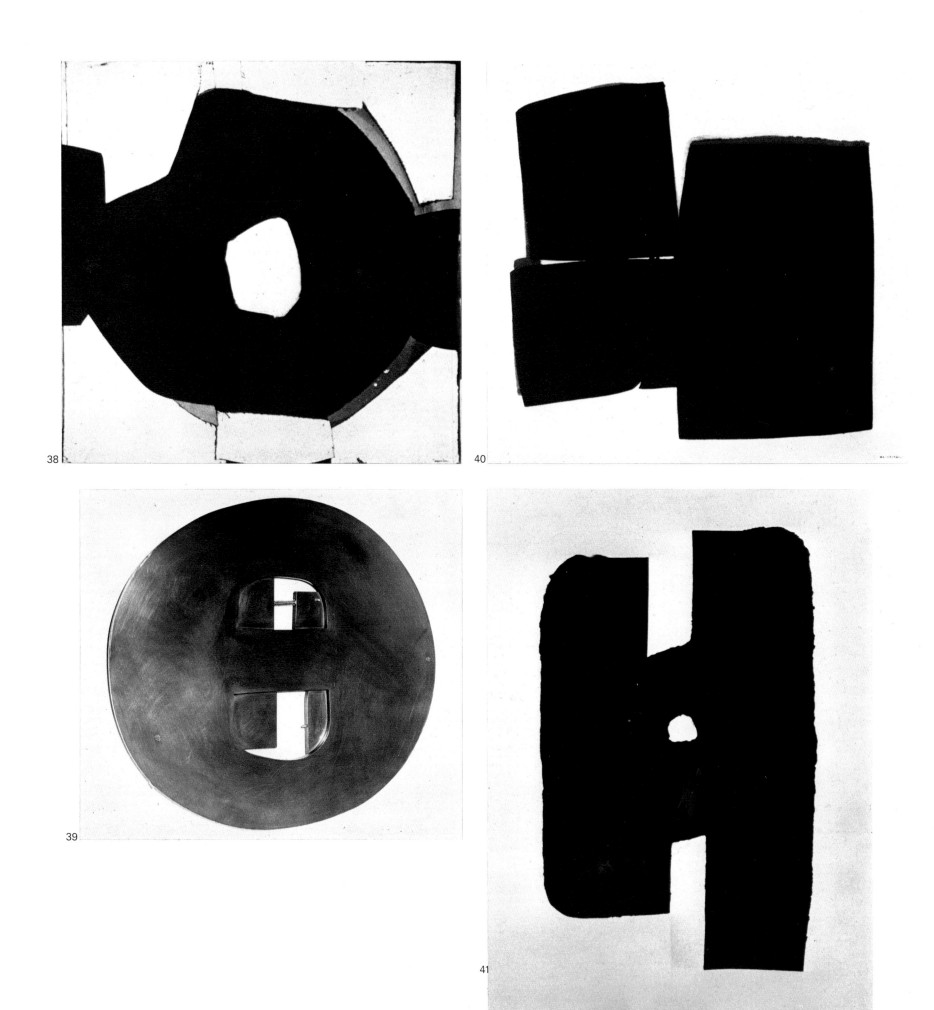

38

39

40

41

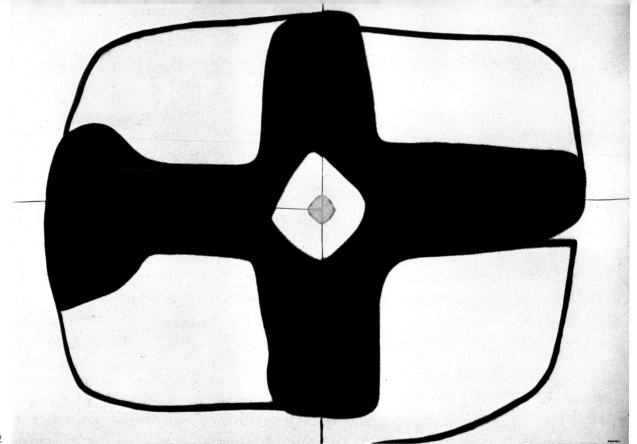

42

42. LL-1-72 in two parts, A & B. 1972. Painted canvas collage, 240 × 348 cm.

their ability to discover a symbolic value in these forms has certainly helped us to analyse the possible "intrinsic forma-tiveness" —we might almost call it visceral— of signs in re-lation to man. And this is where Marca-Relli's *Gestalten* are of extraordinary value, acquiring a polyvalent significance with real physiological power, for they come from man him-self; they are the result of a real isomorphism which justi-fies their constant reappearance and their repeated pre-sence. They probably have no specific meaning, but their aesthetic and emblematic value is undeniable.

It is possible that in the case of Marca-Relli, when he resorts in his works to triangles, to the strength of a cross, to the tension of diagonals in a square, to a six-pointed star, to a white angle holding a black angle, to a funnel as a positive facing another funnel which is its negative, to the spokes of a wheel, to the axes of an eccentric, etc., we cannot speak with any great precision of signs in their literal sense; a pre-ferable term might be that of "womb-metaphors", using the word "wombs" as Arthur Koestler does in that absorbing book, *The Act of Creation* (1964), in which he explains the convergence of originally independent series of represen-tations as something essential to creative inspiration. Koest-ler's generalization of this principle, which according to him constitutes the basis of all artistic or scientific discovery, might have a real value in the multifaceted signs of Marca-Relli. These "wombs" can already be found in his earliest compositions. They are in his very heart. They are fragments of those flashing, almost polyphonic rhythms and construc-tions which he brought into play to construct a shifting, dy-namic and gestural "whole". The only thing is that in the gradual process of simplification, of reduction of the forms to their barest essence, he has been left with the sign, the most naked aspect of his "writing", and with it he closes the last stage in his work by creating hieroglyphs which are quite peculiar to him and can be readily identified, for they do not place us on the road of recognition but on that of memory. Not on that of naturalistic images but on that of the "im-ages-of-memory" of Emmanuel Loewy. Images of a schema-tic type, with the force of emblems, which serve us admir-ably as codes that help us to memorize not what we see with our eyes but what we think with our vision.

TALKING TO MARCA-RELLI

The best way of getting right inside Marca-Relli's work is to be able to know him personally, in his studio-workshop, at his home. His human vitality as a person is as evident when he is working as when he is vehemently expounding his ideas. He is not —nor does he wish to be— one of those many, many artists who justify their work with their words. Marca-Relli speaks without any difficulty, with fluid phrases and clear ideas, but in the end, when it is a question of his own work, he prefers to let it speak for itself, to let his pictures clarify his words rather than the reverse, as has so often occurred. The function of the painter's words is to clarify, not to define, to situate, not to explain, to elucidate, not to justify. In the case of Marca-Relli, however, his words become more interesting on account of the inner coherence of his ideas, the experience he shows in formulating a logical thought — probably acquired when he was lecturing at Yale and Berkeley — and, above all, the manifest interest he has always shown in following a sort of logic in harmony with his life and his work.

The paragraphs transcribed below have been taken from the long tape-recorded conversations we held in Marca-Relli's studio-cum-residence at Punta Martinet, in Ibiza, where the painter and his wife, Anita, spend most of their time, in a splendid house in a development planned by the Catalan architect Josep Lluís Sert, once president of the C.I.A.M. and former Dean of the Harvard School of Architecture.

In Ibiza Marca-Relli feels rested and serene, relaxed, spontaneous. The pressures of modern civilization and the angst of city life seem very far away. The idyllic life of a white island, with a pure sea and an uncontaminated sky, stimulates his work. And he works constantly, taking advantage of every minute of sunlight that lets him enjoy to the full the serene tranquillity of his studio.

His studio commands a sweeping view over the whole bay of the town of Ibiza. Aeroplanes fly right over the huddled mass of the old walled capital on their way to the airport. The sunsets transform the tones of the light in his studio. In this setting, in August 1974 and in the intervals between several of his latest pictures, I had the interesting conversations with Marca-Relli that produced the ideas I have transcribed below: perhaps the most suitable way to close a book on his work. For during these conversations Marca-Relli explained his existential philosophy, his aesthetic and his practice of that aesthetic. He recalled different events in his life and confessed ideals. Always in front of his work, past or present, constantly referring to it, though without trying either to foreshadow or to interpret it; only wanting, at most, to clarify the intention to communicate that is in his pictures. Here, then, we have Marca-Relli in person.

"Painting has nothing to do with imitating life. It has its own life; in it reality is based on its own rules."

"I regard painting as the solution to a problem, perhaps an insoluble problem, never totally solved; for this reason one goes on painting."

"I live in the shadow of boredom. Work is my only escape. The worst crime a painting can commit is to be boring."

"At that time (in 1940) the American artist was completely cut out of society, while in Europe the artist still managed to keep some tie with society, teaching, poster work, shows, etc. The American artist was a 'new' being in the American environment."

"Cubism had come close to making out of space a formula, almost an academy. Analytical Cubism had opened the door to a new aesthetic, but it had also shut it."

"The words 'originality' and 'new' are not in the involvement of the creative act —these are words used, as it were, looking in— the critics, the museums, the establishment may use these words to describe an artist or his work, but to the artist, involved in the creative process, these words are meaningless. The artist can only think in terms of self-expression, of personal contributions, or of discovery."

"In a painting the positive forces can only be so with the consciousness of the negative forces, and so it is with the positive and negative spaces in a painting. The way they co-exist becomes the tension and force of the painting. All positive acts would be meaningless without the intervention of the negative. All the dripping or brushstrokes in a painting become only valid in relation to the negative spaces —otherwise they are just acts— meaningless."

"First we have to recognize that we do not want to copy nature, a painting is not a reproduction of natural objects. An exciting painting exists by itself, it must contain elements of strength, contradiction, imbalance, etc.; it must create an interest."

"I feel a desire to destroy the central subject or theme, so that the solution itself may become pure delight."

"By creating forms, not unrelated forms but human forms, the figure no longer exists at a naturalistic level, only at an emotional one."

"Collage disciplines my way of thinking, it leads me to work in terms of forms, outlines, imaginary spaces. In this way I do not fall into the temptation of thinking that nature is a reality. I think of painting as an intrinsic reality and this is my greatest concern."

"What is true in nature is not necessarily true on a two-dimensional canvas. It is an illusory reality."

"There is a logic in nature, which we feel; there is also a logic in painting, which sometimes escapes us. It is not easy to understand it or define it, but we feel that it exists."

"What is inconceivable and absurd in nature is conceivable in painting; it exists insofar as the painter has created it. Suddenly he gives it a new sense of reality, which is a reality of painting. This is where the strength of the painting begins to exist."

"Life is reality. A painting can be real in itself as nature is. If a painting is transformed into pure objectivity it cancels itself, for it becomes nature once more."

"The painting must exist by virtue of its own merits, its own associations. It must stimulate the viewer so that he may understand these things which are so surprising, these possibilities which are so opposed."

"I am very much aware of the 'edges' of a form. For the edge of a form indicates where a central volume is surrounded by an outer volume. It is at the border that this meeting takes place. What may happen at that edge is very important, depending on how it is found, how it coexists."

"Some elements are more important than others. If you paint a coffee-pot and a cup on a table, the most important thing about the coffee-pot and the cup will not be their visual aspect but the way in which these forms are reflected on the others, the way in which the handle of the coffee-pot suddenly becomes more important than the rest of the pot. It suddenly becomes a live, solid, real contour."

"I have never seen the border-line between what is called non-objective painting and figurative painting, because for me they have always been one and the same thing."

"I believe that when the values or directions of painting change, it must be the painter who perceives it; let the critics come later."

"I think that painters should be free to experiment. And that during their experimenting they should be alone, without any interference from critics, museums or galleries, in order to see whether what they are doing is good or not."

"I have concentrated my life in one direction, which is something I find very normal, for if one finds a pictorial language all one wants to do is to study this language in order to see more clearly."

"Painting for me is like a mathematical problem, an obsessive problem that I have to solve. I face the problem and ask myself, for instance, if it is possible to make this figurative, or with a less figurative idea, and then I try to see how far I can go in order to see this reality and what it means."

"In my painting I may use different themes, I may use a figure or not, but if I do use a figure I always regard it as a form that can be alive, that can exist in space. Then I may or may not use colour; it doesn't matter. All that does matter to me is the problem of space."

"A period in which everything has worked out well for me is a period that no longer interests me, because the problem is solved."

"When I look at the things I painted over twenty years ago, I feel even more certain that there is no evolution. Then I had certain problems which I solved more or less correctly, and now I am endeavouring to solve today's problems properly. But I cannot say that I have perfected a technique or that I have a clearer idea of painting after twenty years."

"Pictorial ideas may be quite clear when I paint them, and then they become utterly confused again."

"The whole process of my work starts with the reinterpretation of a figure in a plastic sense, within an idea of construction of the picture, for I have never practised realism."

"The old idea of anatomy does not interest me, for it includes a lot of worthless things. I only want things that can contribute to solving the picture. The figure is an ambiguous form, for in it there are all the possible forms. That is why it is such a challenge to painting itself."

"There is another reality besides that of nature. What may be clear in a picture is not clear at all in nature; hence the difference."

"I do not work with an a priori intellectual idea. I try to make the plastic language express everything one wants; that is why it is a work that does not know where it is heading; one cannot have a fixed idea to start with."

"It is easier for me to do something that has a natural symbolism (a wheel, for instance) than to make an image that gives you the sense of the force existing in the human figure,

for this force may change, and so it demands a continuous search for expression, for the true imaginary figure."

"In my opinion naturalism in painting does not exist, for naturalism is nothing but a copy of nature, it cannot be art. Italian Renaissance art—all ancient art, indeed—is pure image, abstract."

"When I finish a picture which I regard as figurative, it must be a figure in such a way that one is conscious of a presence, of an emotion, but not of a figure. The figure must become something else, a pure human sense of a presence" (1).

* * *

There are hardly any limits to Marca-Relli's eloquence, his passion for dialogue, his eagerness to elucidate and explain in detail his experiences and opinions. The hours go by placidly in the incomparable silence of the serene, peaceful white island. And Marca-Relli will go on painting, thinking, sometimes writing down his ideas or reflections, for to him living means painting, and painting forms part of life itself.

(1) In order to complete some of the concepts he had expressed personally in Ibiza, I have also resorted to his "personal jottings", which are of extraordinary interest, to the particularly important interview he gave to Ralph Hyams and to the interviews with Gladys Kashdin and Antonio Bernabeu, the latter for the Spanish review Gaceta del Arte.

43. Ora (5-54-16). 1953. Oil and collage, 50.5 × 45.5 cm.

44. F-S-17-66. 1966. Oil and canvas collage, 48.3 × 38 cm.

45. F-S-7-67. 1967. Oil and canvas collage, 55.3 × 45.8 cm.

46. F-S-12-67. 1967. Oil and canvas collage, 58.2 × 47.6 cm.

43

45

44

46

Recent works

47. Cunard (L - 9 - 62).
1962. Painted vinyl
collage on wood,
190.5 × 162.5 cm.

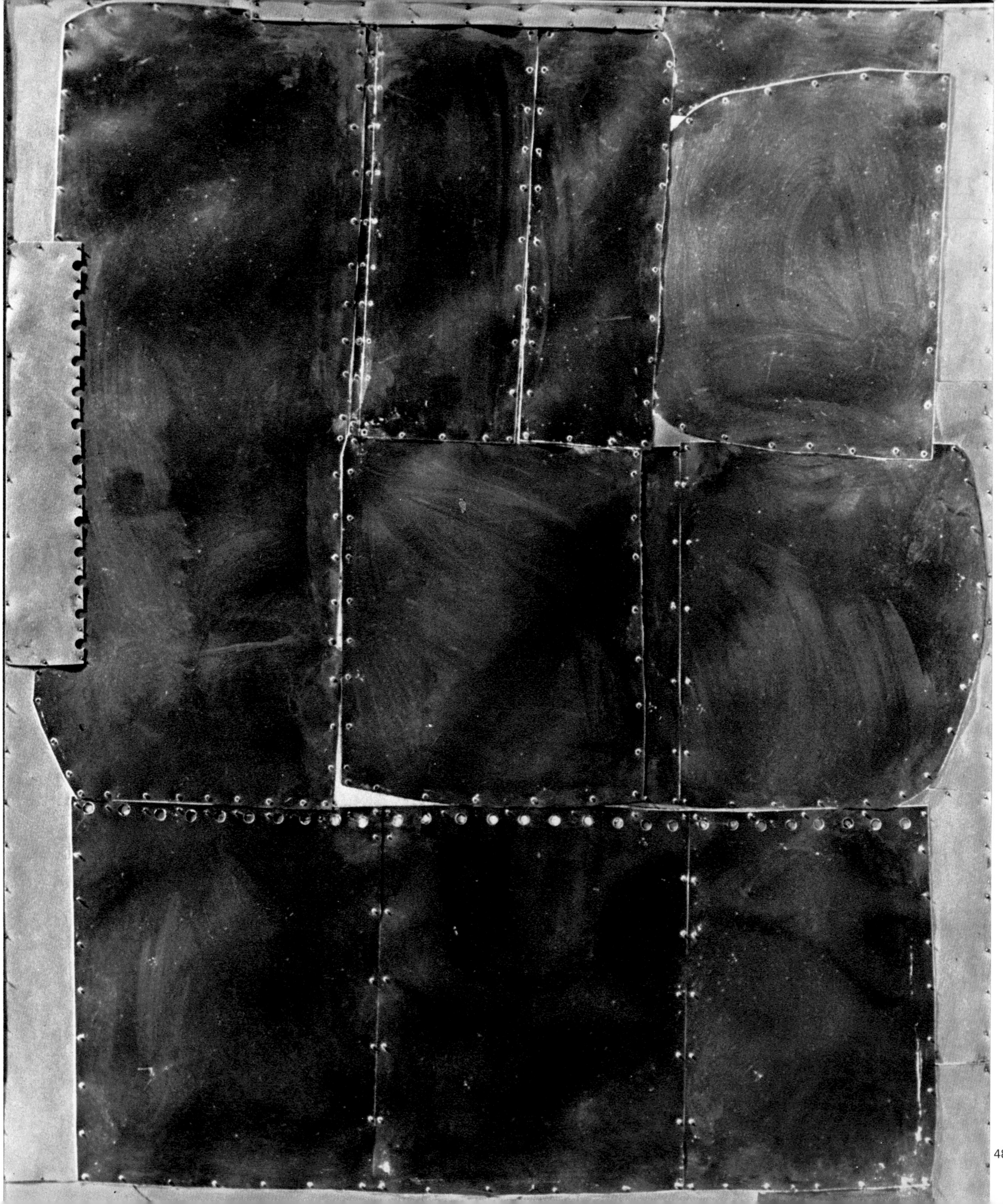

48

48. Engine Room D (L-11-62). 1962. Painted vinyl collage on painted wood, 161 × 188 cm.

49. Room B-3 (L-7-62). 1962. Vinyl plastic, 198 × 121.5 cm.

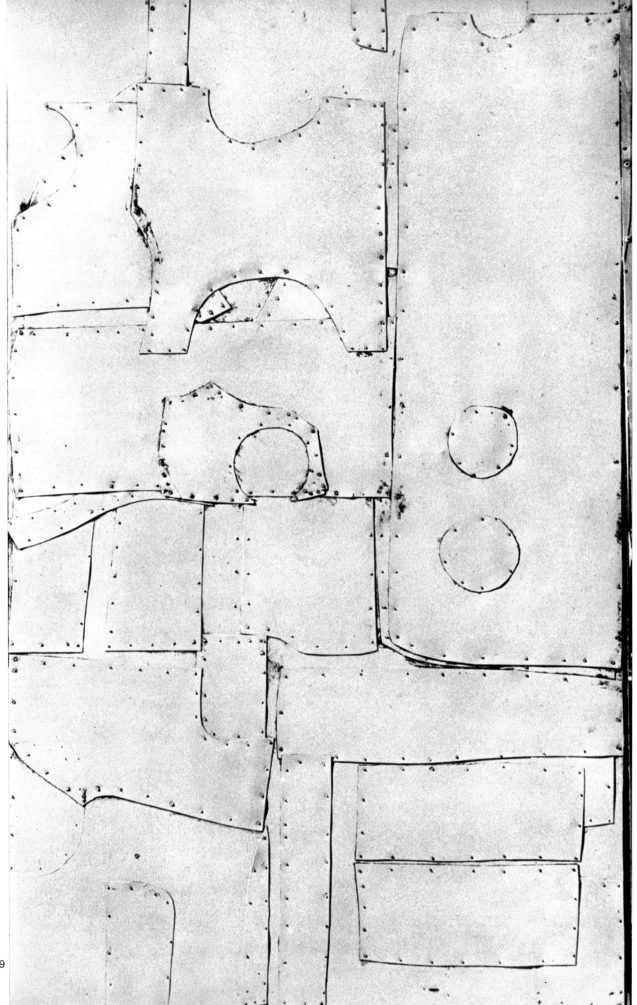

49

50. Plan M (L-5-62). 1962. Painted vinyl collage, 182.5 × 152.4 cm.

51. Cristóbal (L-12-62). 1962. Painted vinyl collage, 190.5 × 162.5 cm.

50

51

52. Plan B (L-6-62). 1962. Painted vinyl collage, 182.5 × 152.5 cm.

53. Exit 4 (L-10-62). 1962. Painted vinyl collage, 188 × 161 cm.

54. Untitled (M-1-63). 1963. Painted aluminium collage, 89 × 94 cm.

55. Pilot (L-10-63). 1963. Painted aluminium collage, 160 × 190.5 cm.

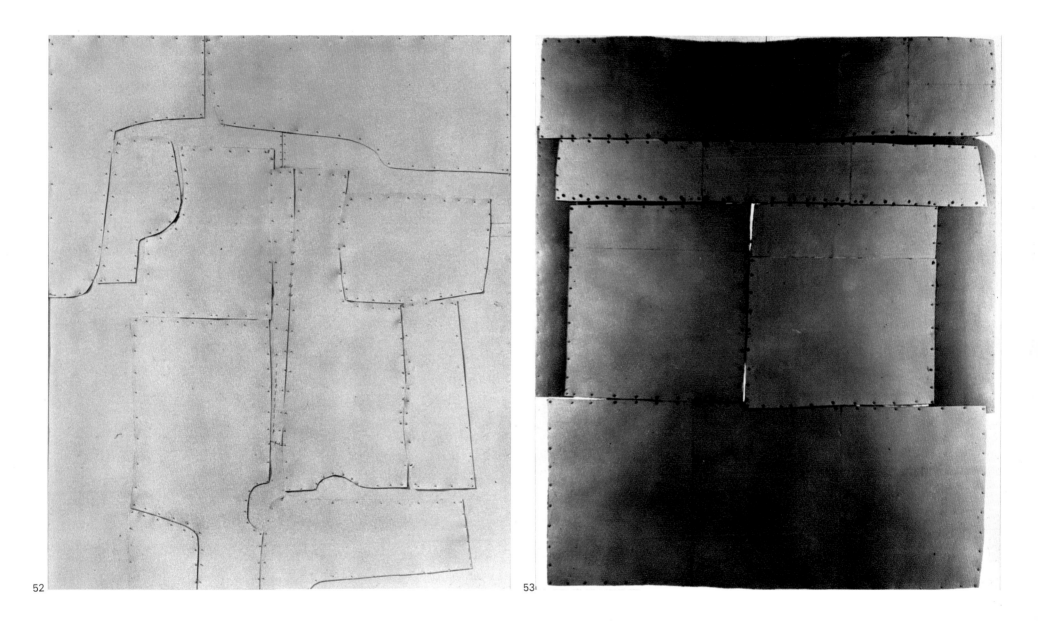

52

53

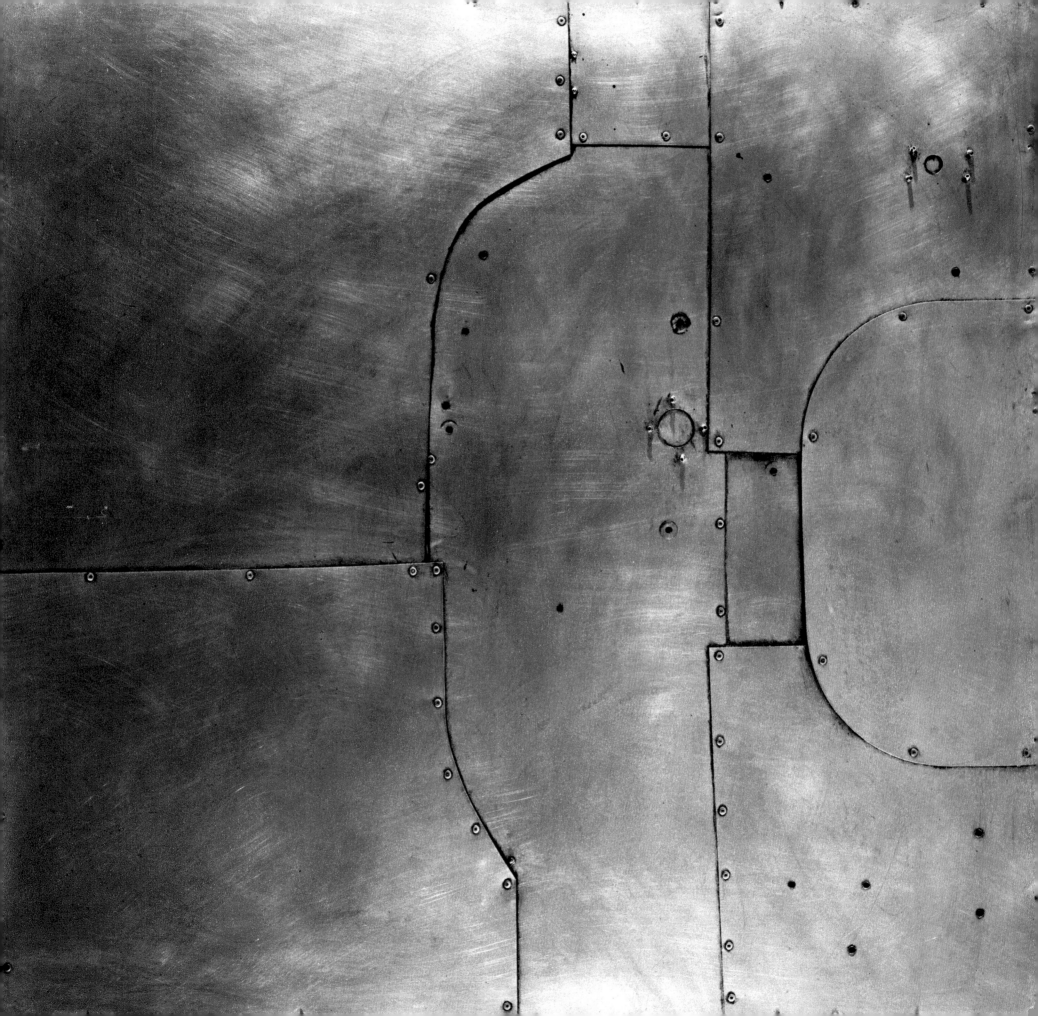

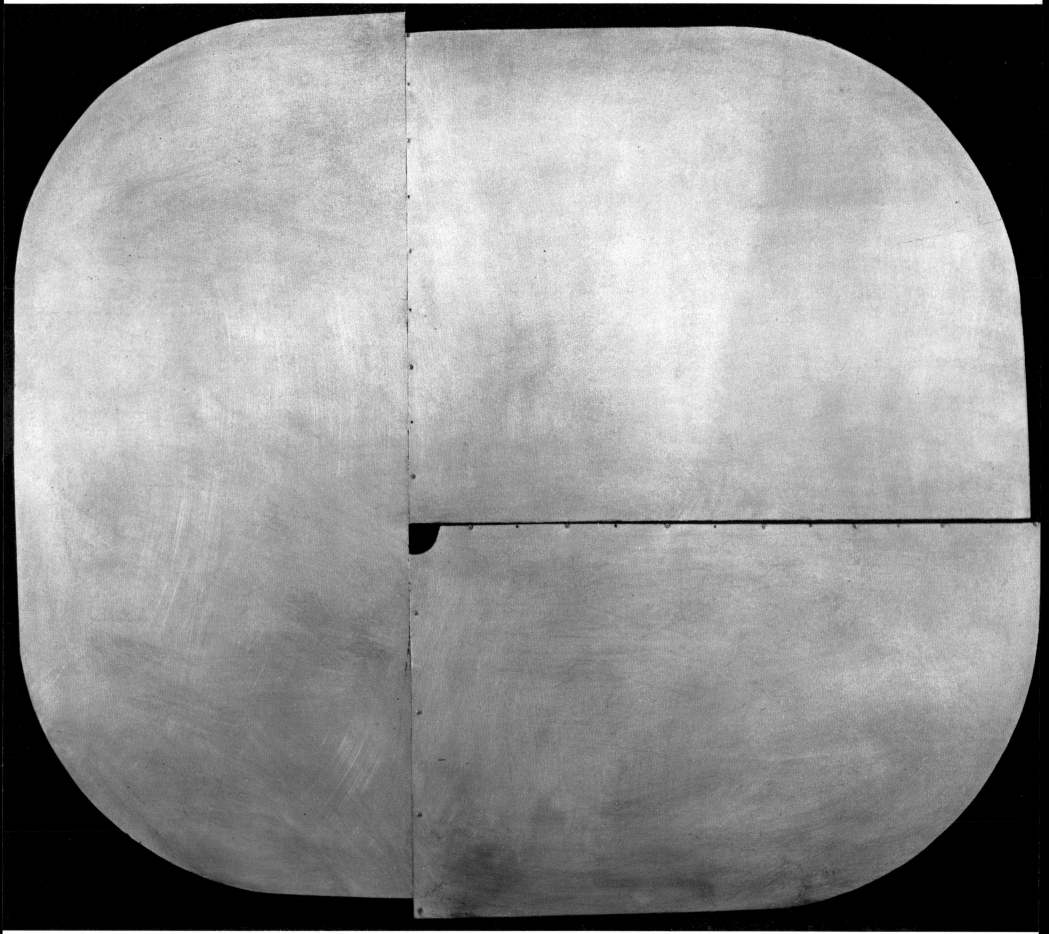

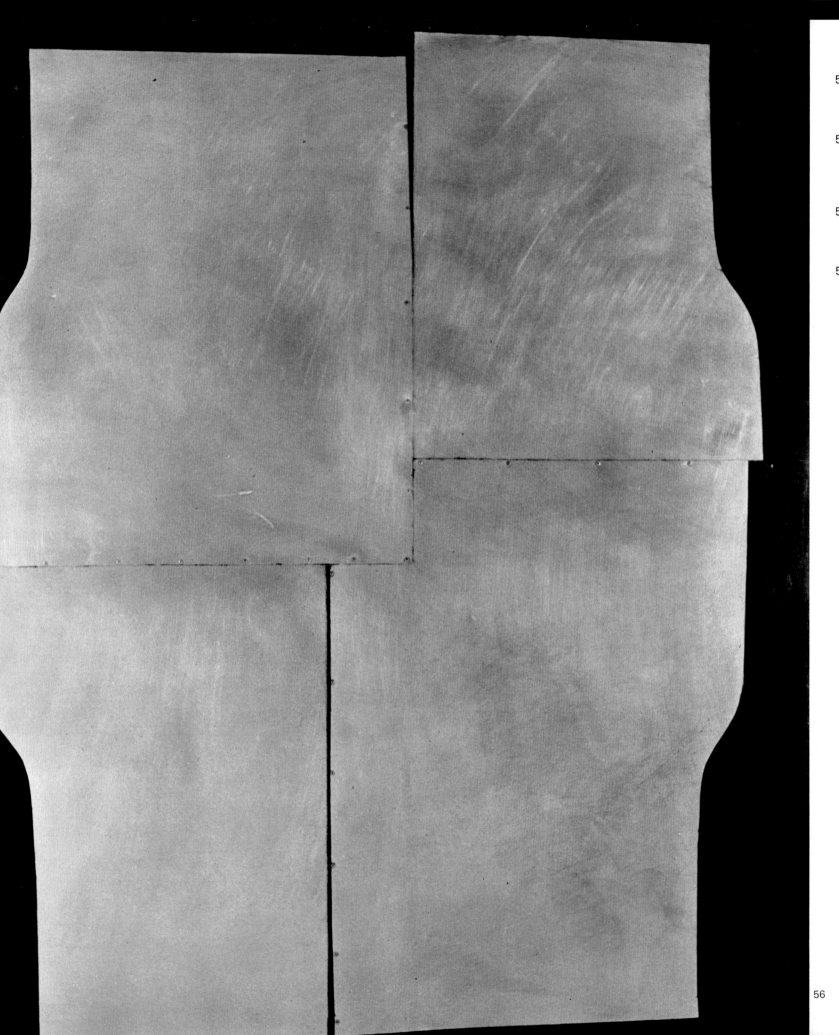

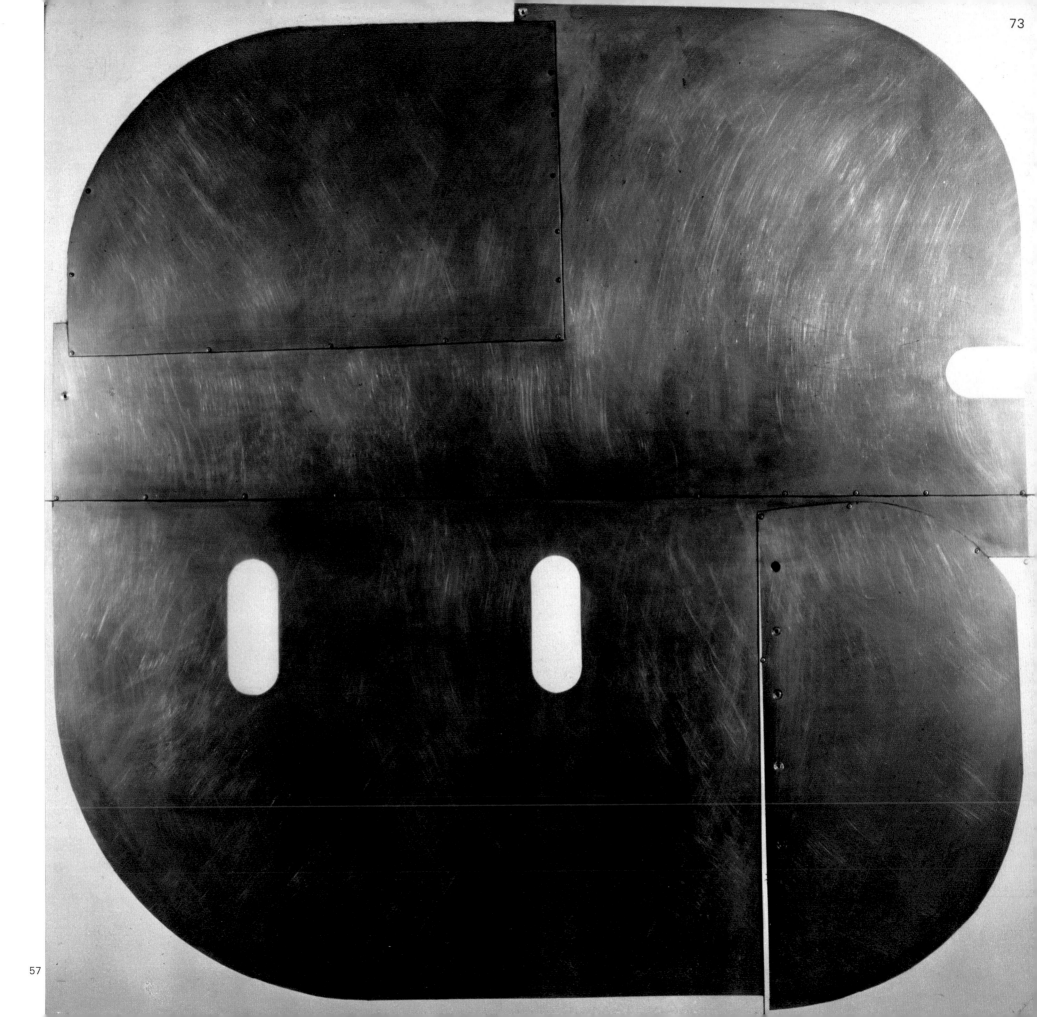

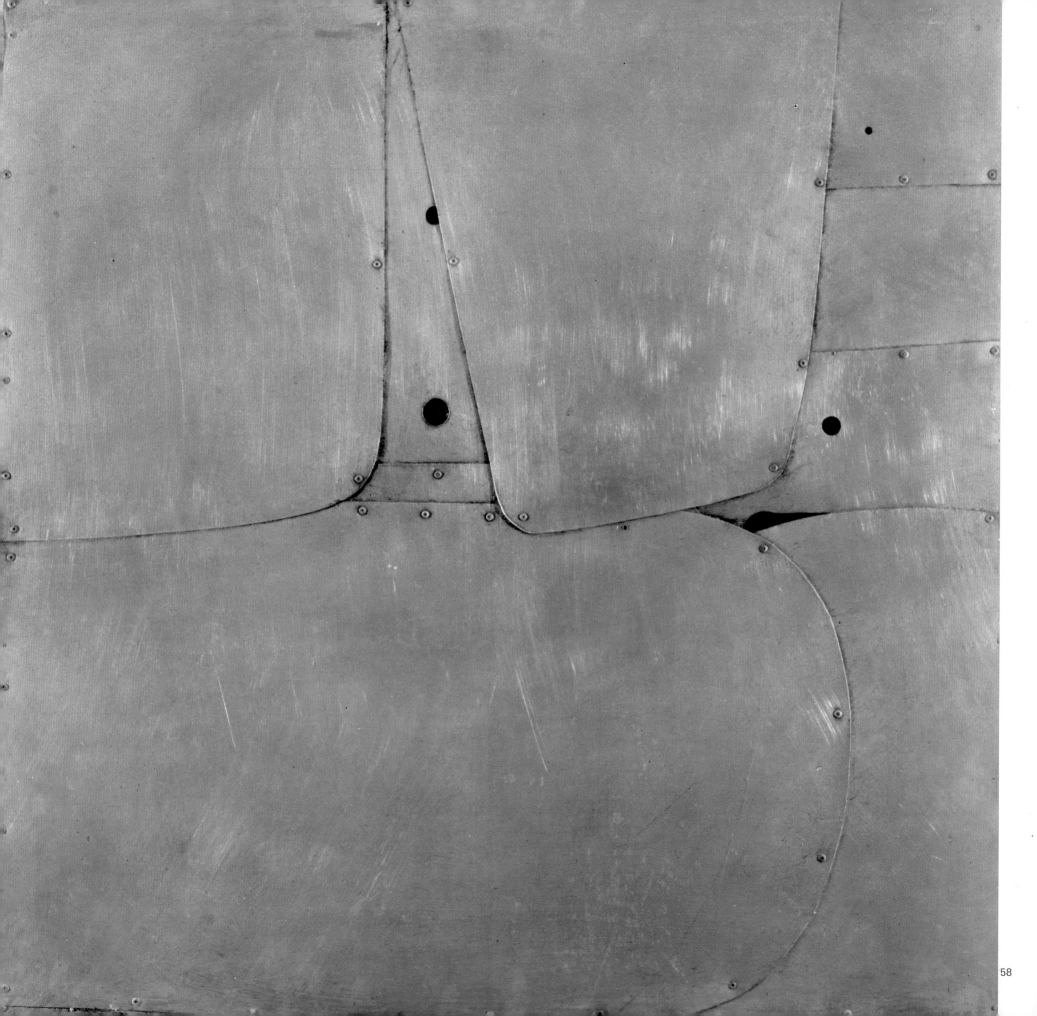

58

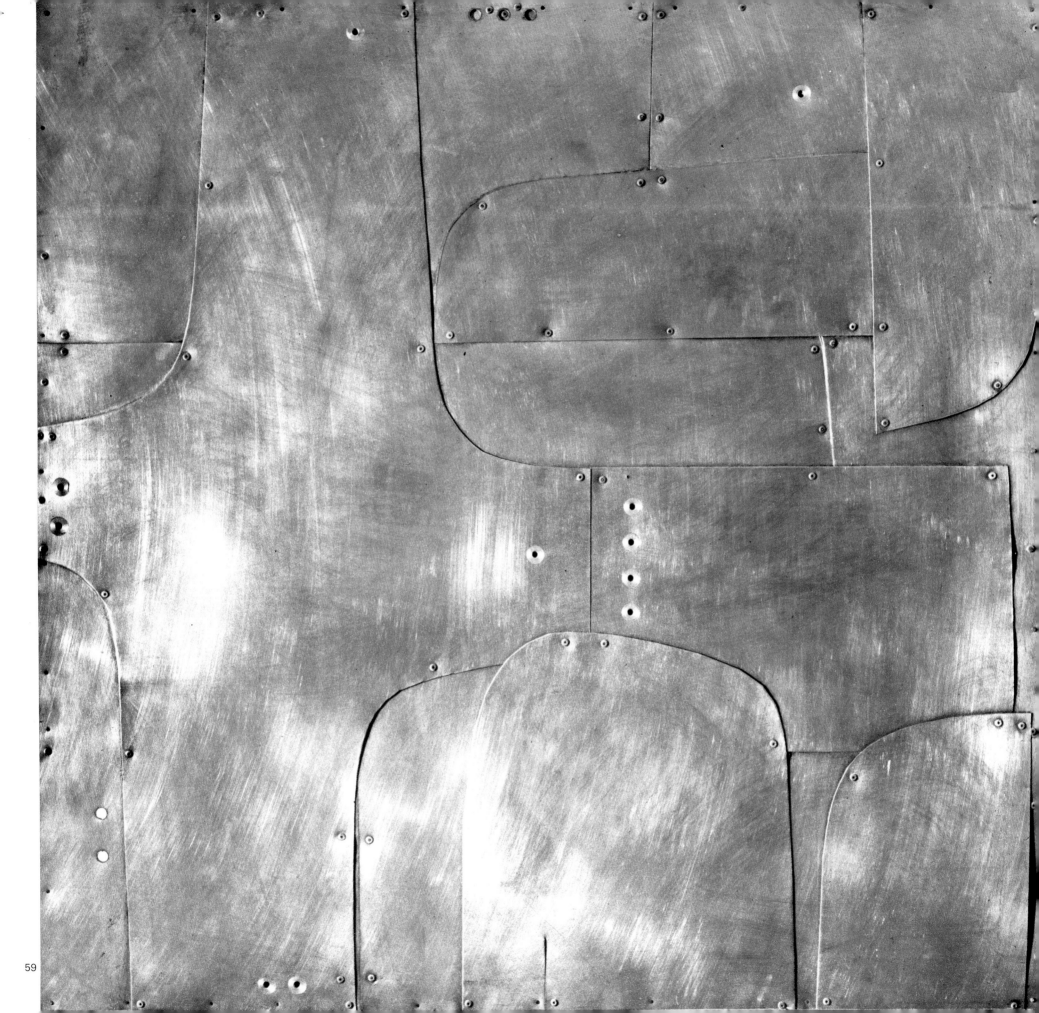

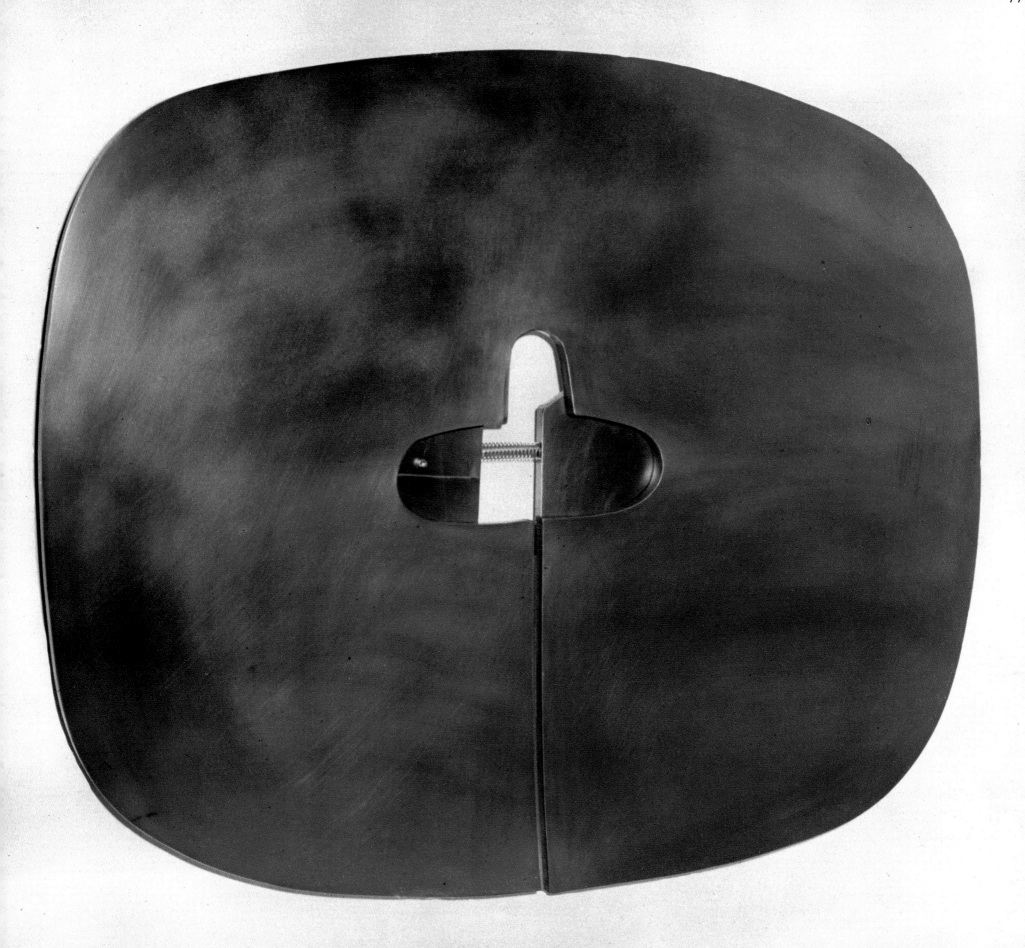

64

64. TR-7 (S-C-P6-66). 1966. Aluminium sculpture, 142 × 122 × 17.5 cm.

65. Q.L. 20-63. 1963. Aluminium collage, 160 × 177.5 cm.

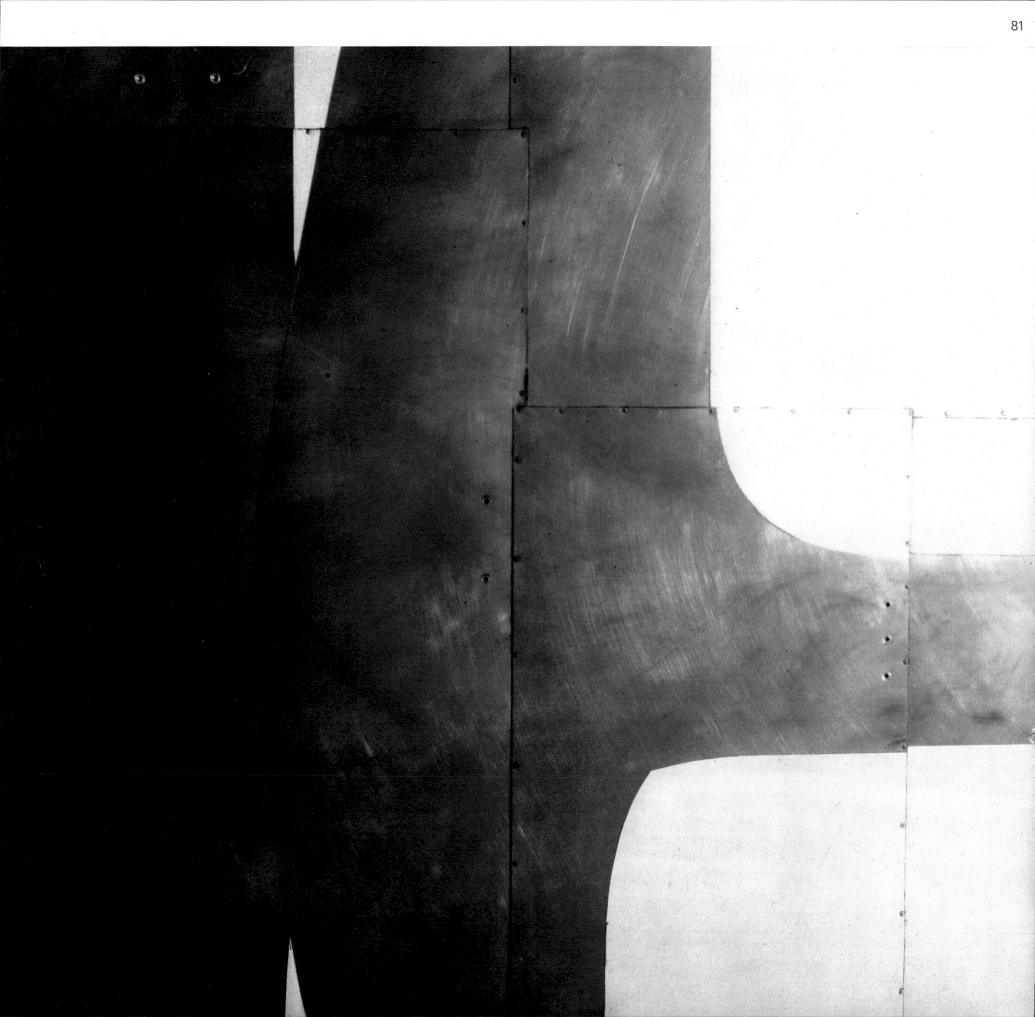

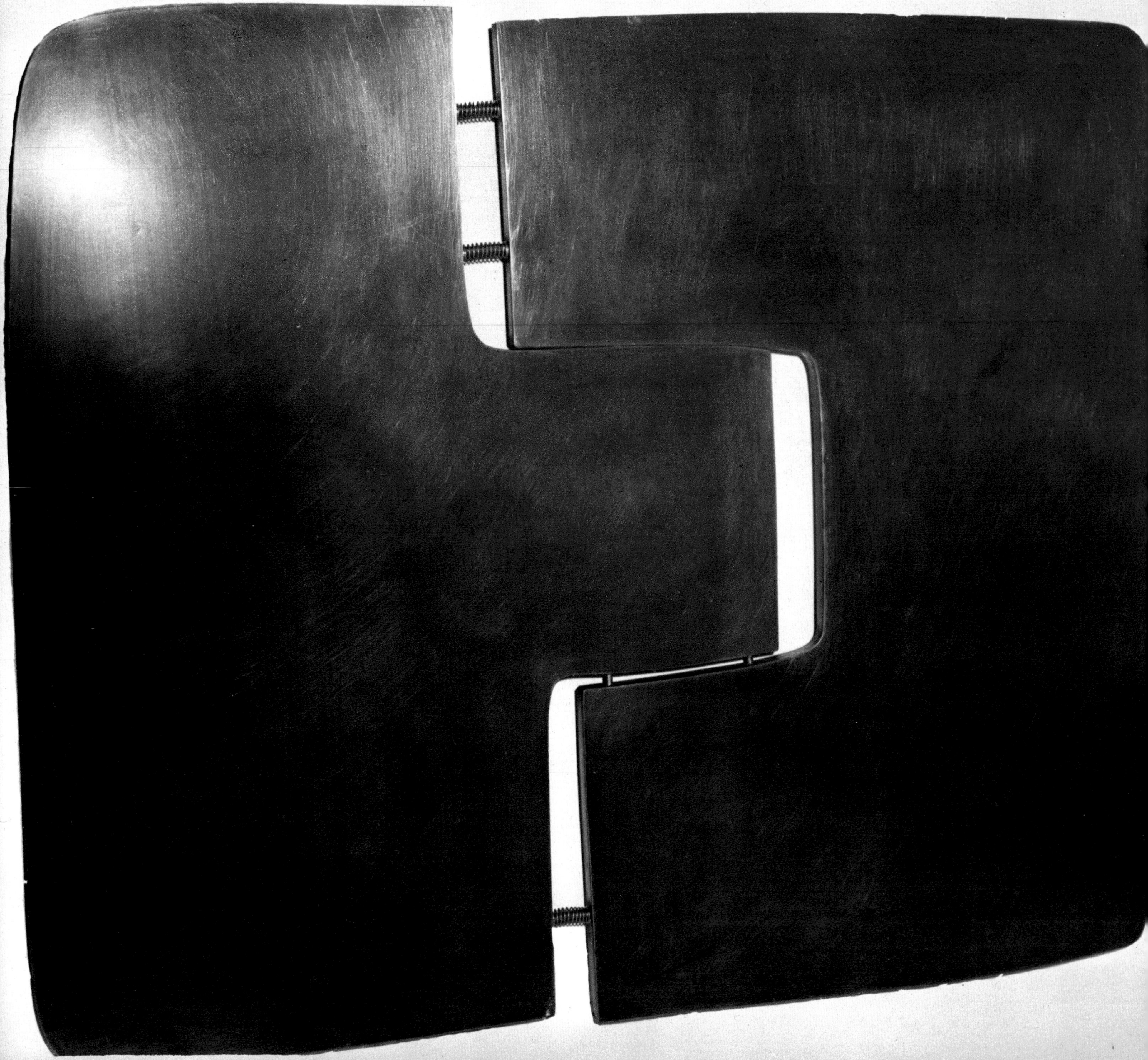

66. Untitled (XL-11-64). 1964. Aluminium relief, 134.5 × 165 cm. Whitney Museum of American Art.

67. Sculpture 1 (S-C-P-1). 1969. Marble and slate, 37 × 37 × 2 cm. Private collection.

67

68. U-4. 1966. Aluminium sculpture, 122 × 142 × 17 cm.

69. XS-1-67. 1967. Canvas collage, 61 × 61 cm. Alfred Schmela Collection, Düsseldorf.

68

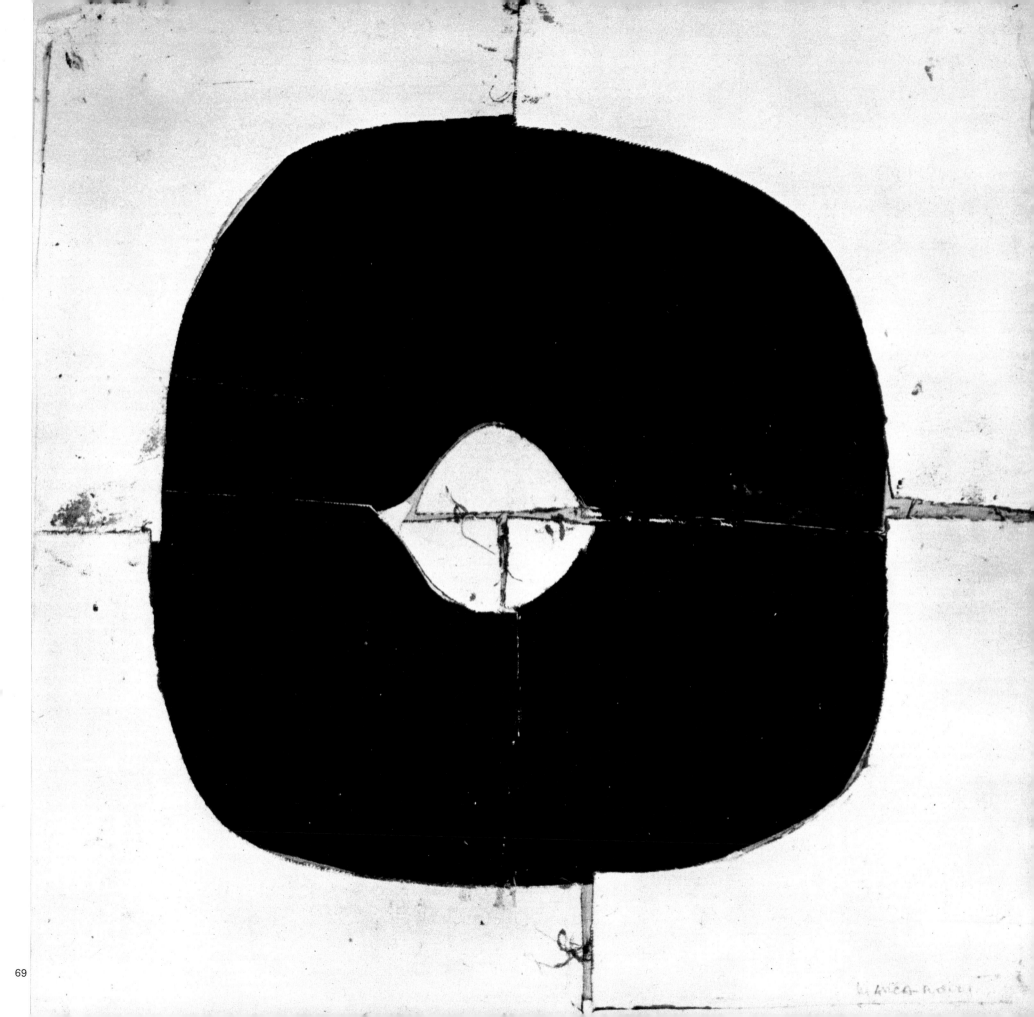

70. L-2-66. 1966. Canvas collage, 183 × 152.5 cm. Private collection.
71. QM-1-66. 1966. Canvas collage, 96.5 × 114 cm. Private collection.

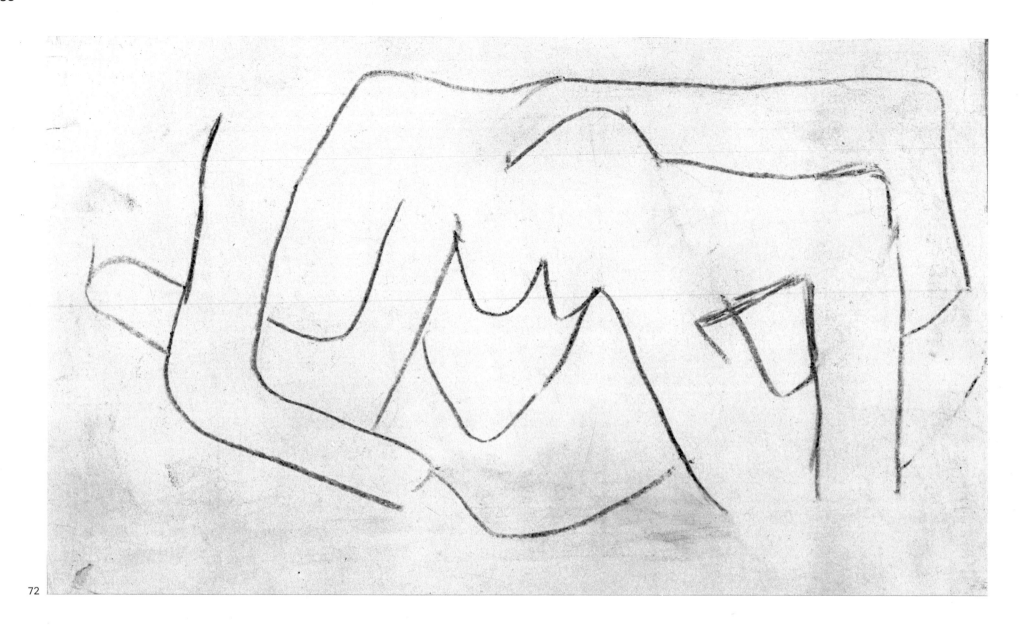

72

72. Drawing.

73. F-M-6-67. 1967. Painted canvas collage, 81 × 91.5 cm.

74. F-M-9-67. 1967. Painted canvas collage, 81 × 91.7 cm.

75. L-16-69. 1969. Canvas collage, 155 × 167.5 cm.

MARER-RELE

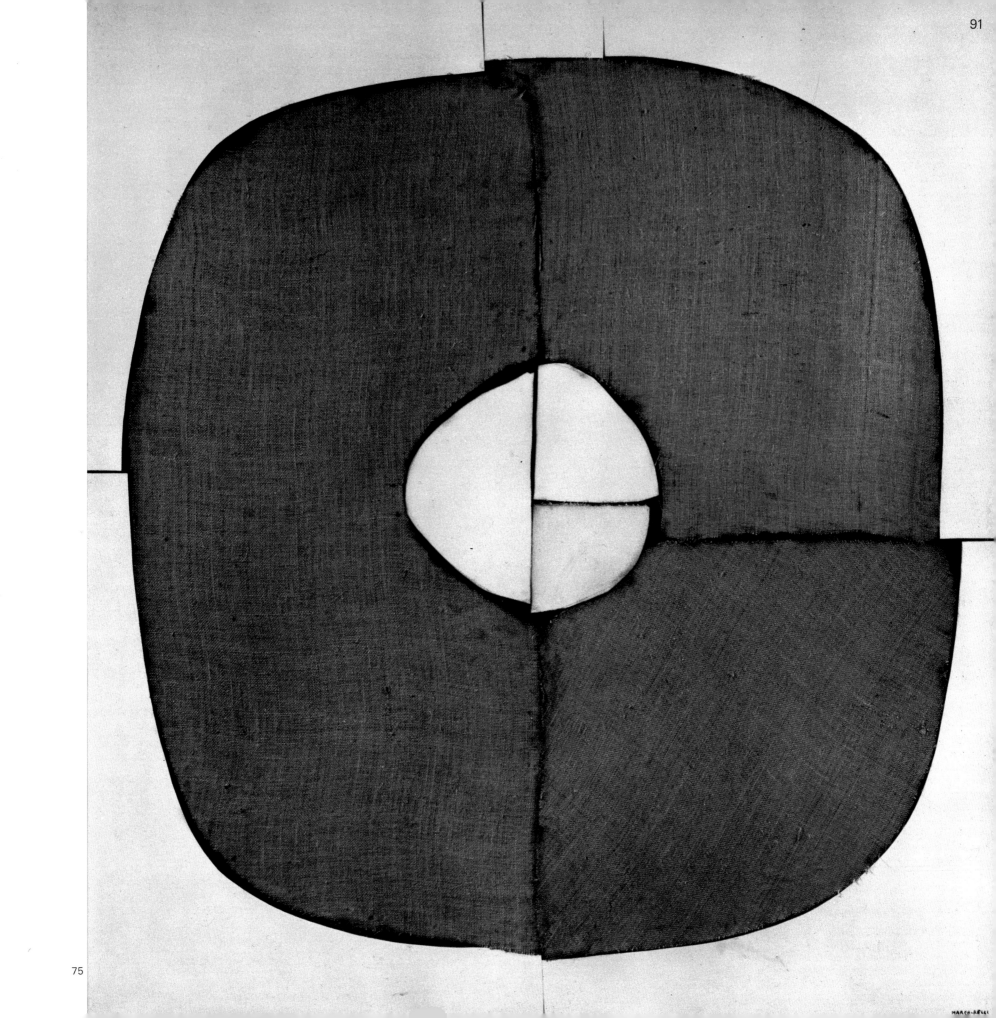

76. F-M-10-67. 1967. Painted canvas collage, 81 × 91.5 cm.

77. Untitled. 1963. Canvas and wax collage, 28.5 × 40.5 cm.

77

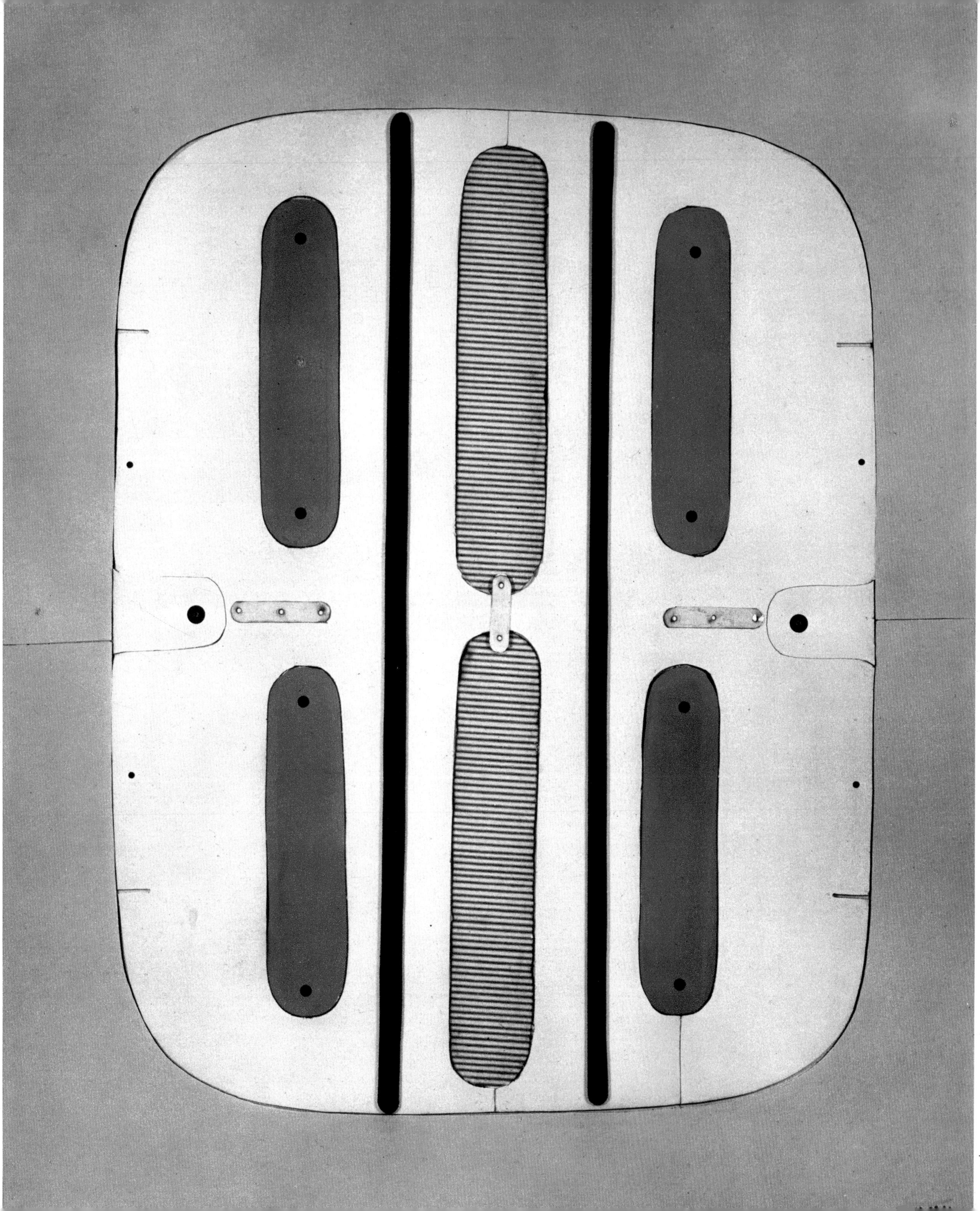

78

78. Image 4 (L-4-69). 1969. Mixed media collage on canvas, 176.5 × 145 cm.

79. Image 18 (L-18-68-69). 1969-1970. Mixed media collage on canvas, 152 × 183 cm. Private collection.

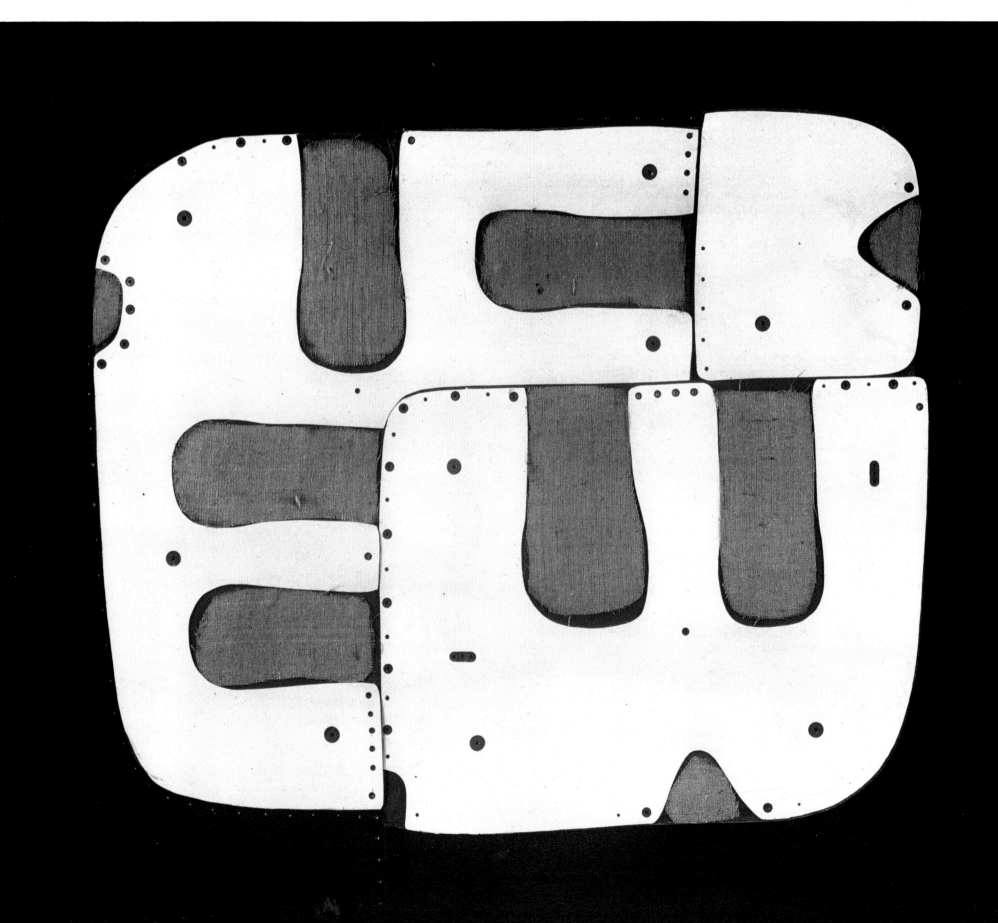

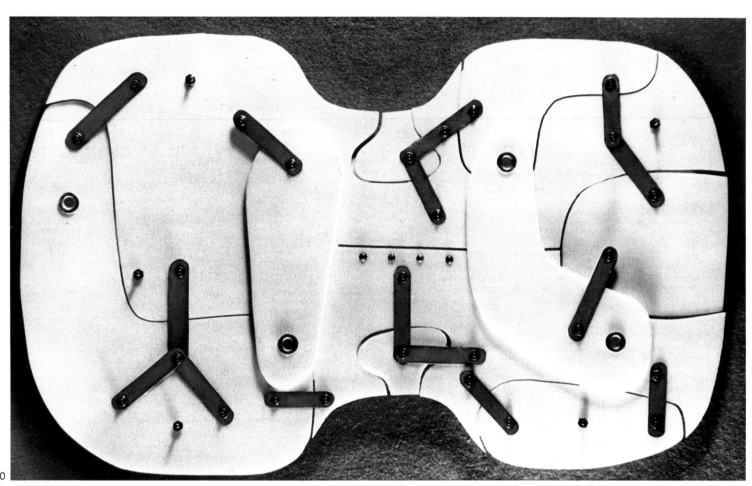

80

80. Untitled relief 1. 1969. Plexiglass. 39.5 × 65 cm.

81. Untitled relief 2. 1969. Plexiglass and wood, 38 × 63.5 cm.

82. L-2-72. 1972. Canvas collage,
176.5 × 144.5 cm.

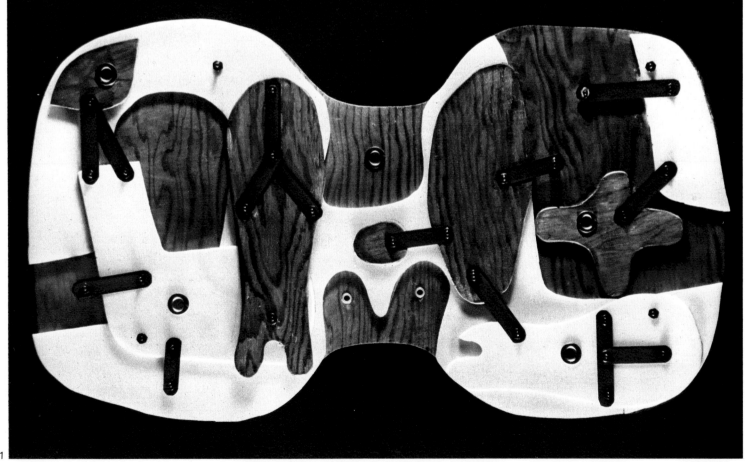

81

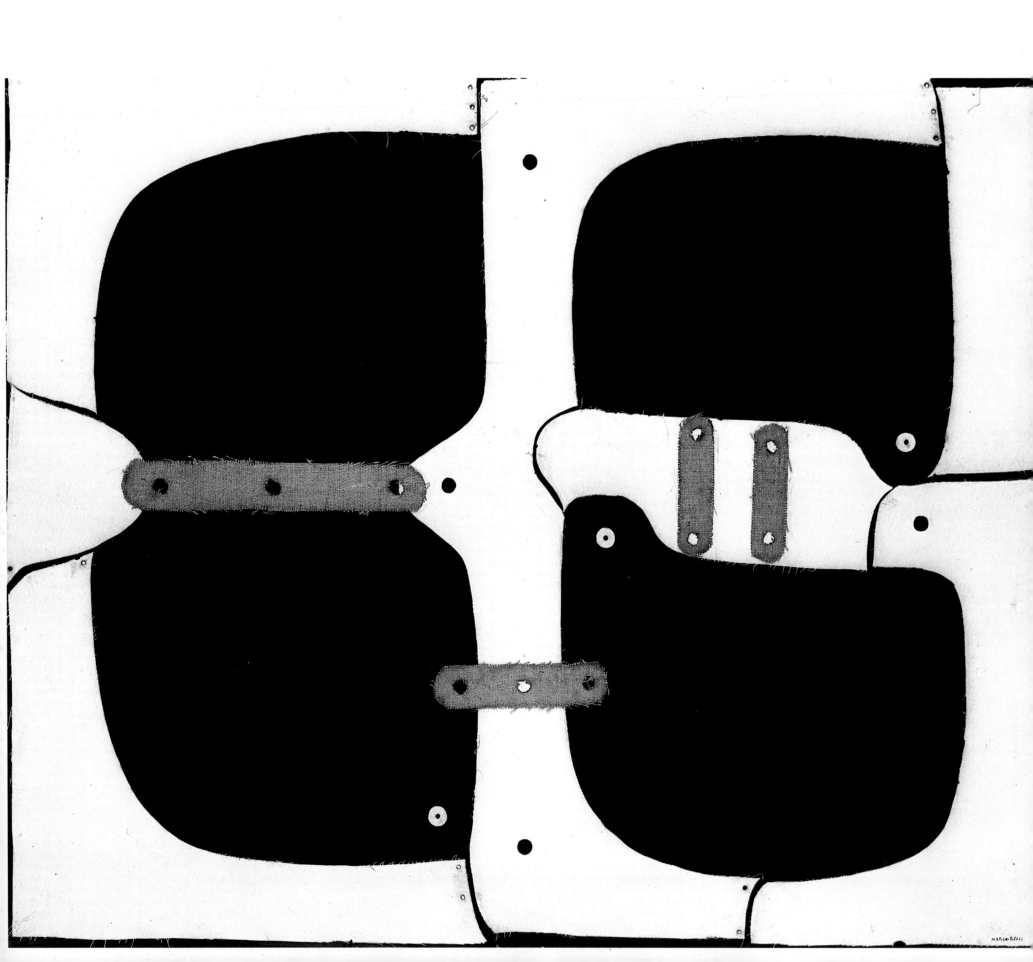

83. L-21-69. 1969. Canvas collage, 147.3 × 181.6 cm.

84. Sculpture 2 (S-C-P-2). Marble and slate, 35 × 13 × 2 cm.

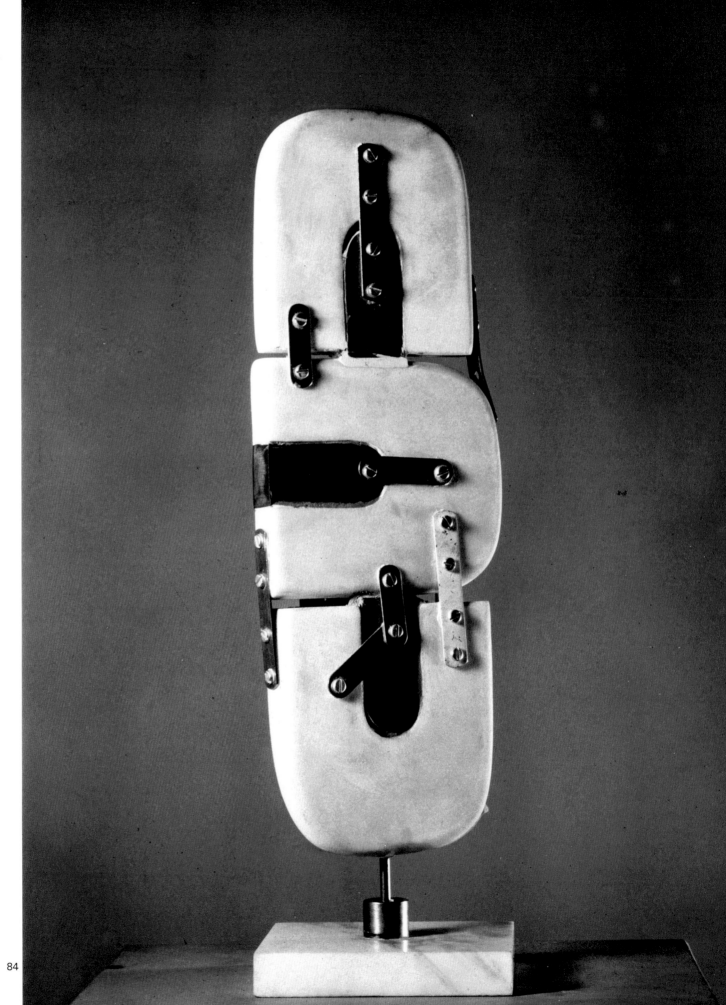

84

85

85. Drawing.

86. L-1-72. 1972. Canvas collage, 155.5 × 175.8 cm.

87. L-4-72. 1972. Canvas collage, 155.5 × 175.8 cm. Private collection.

88. L-3-72. Canvas collage, 156 × 171 cm.

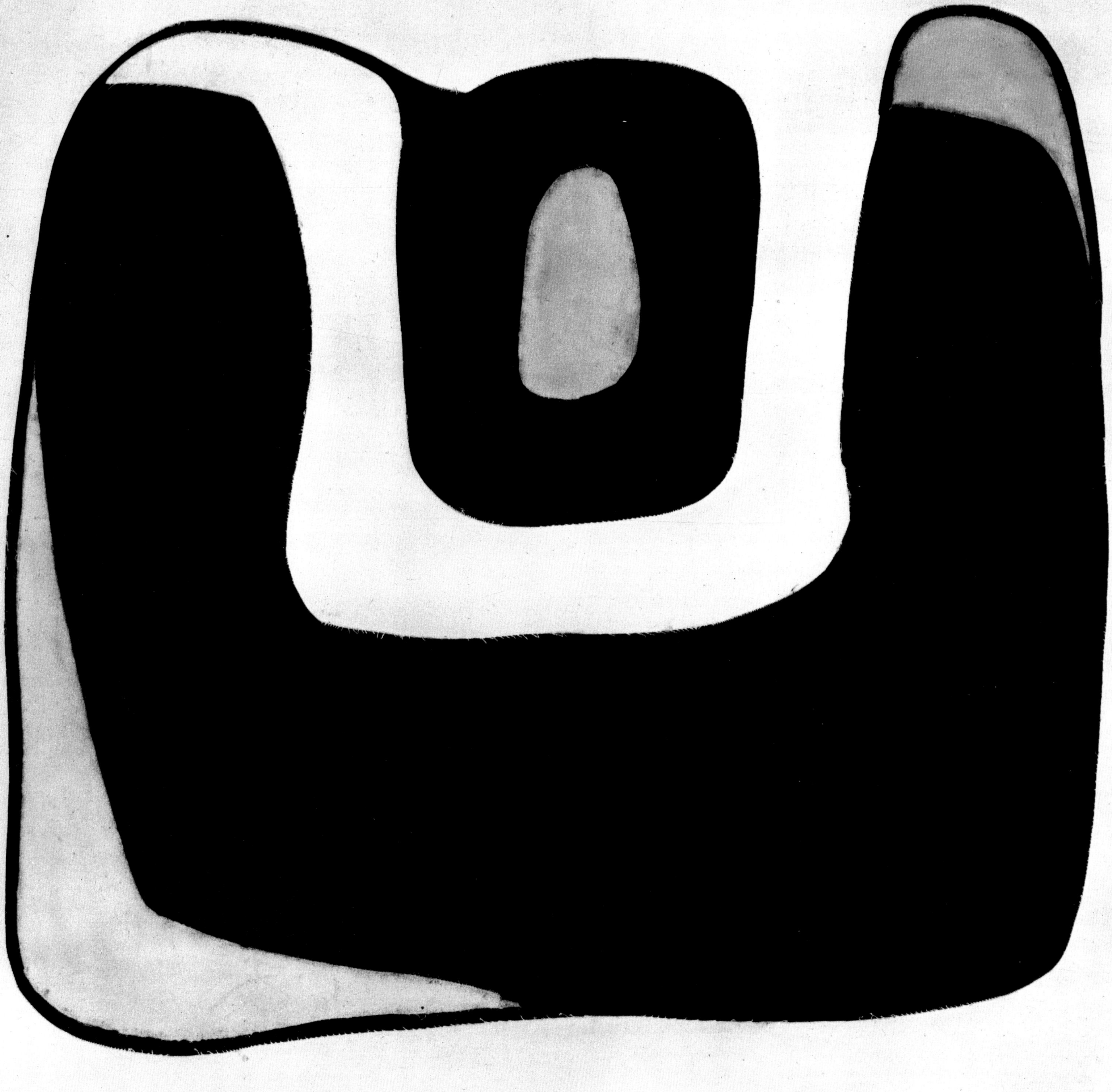

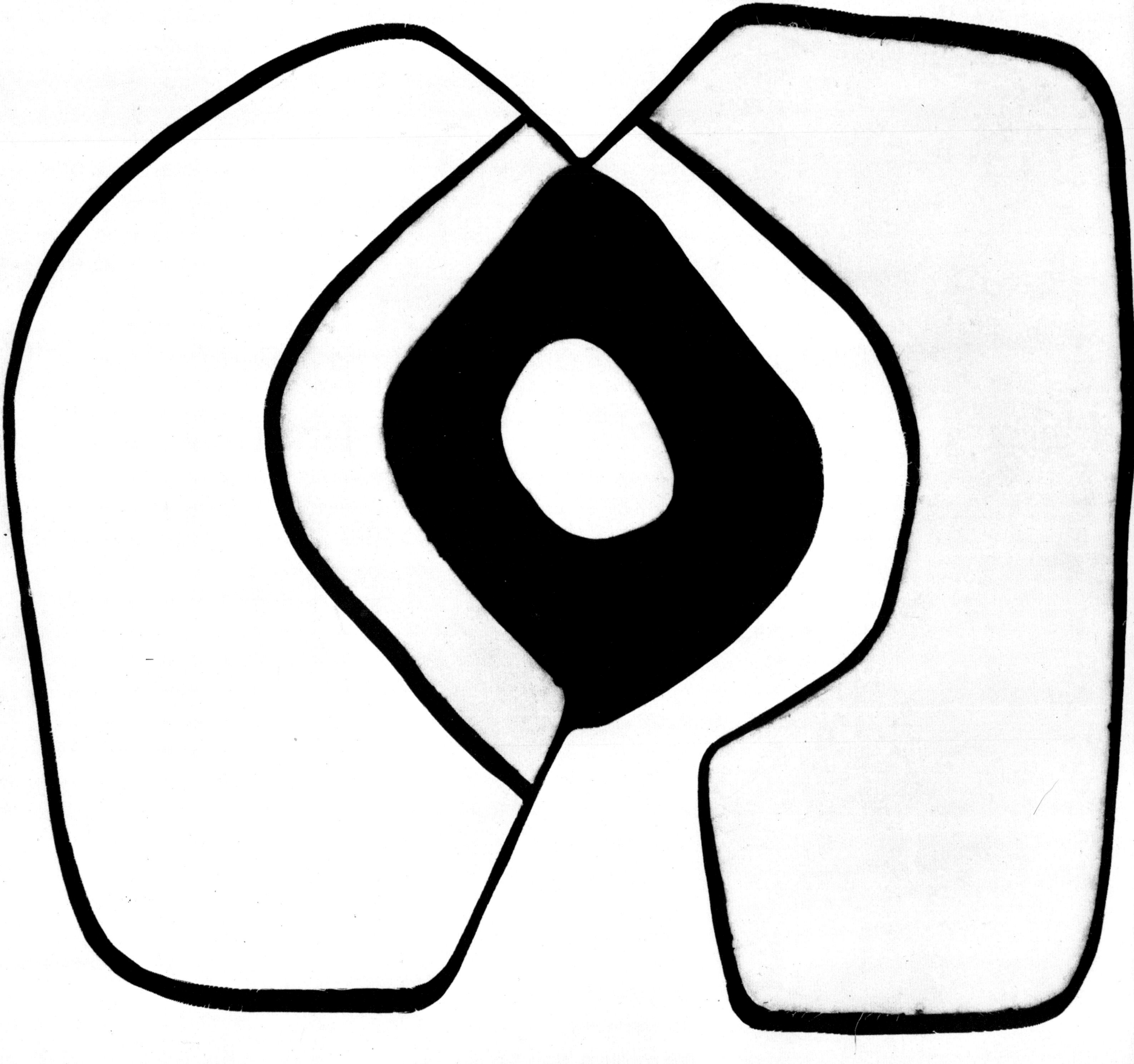

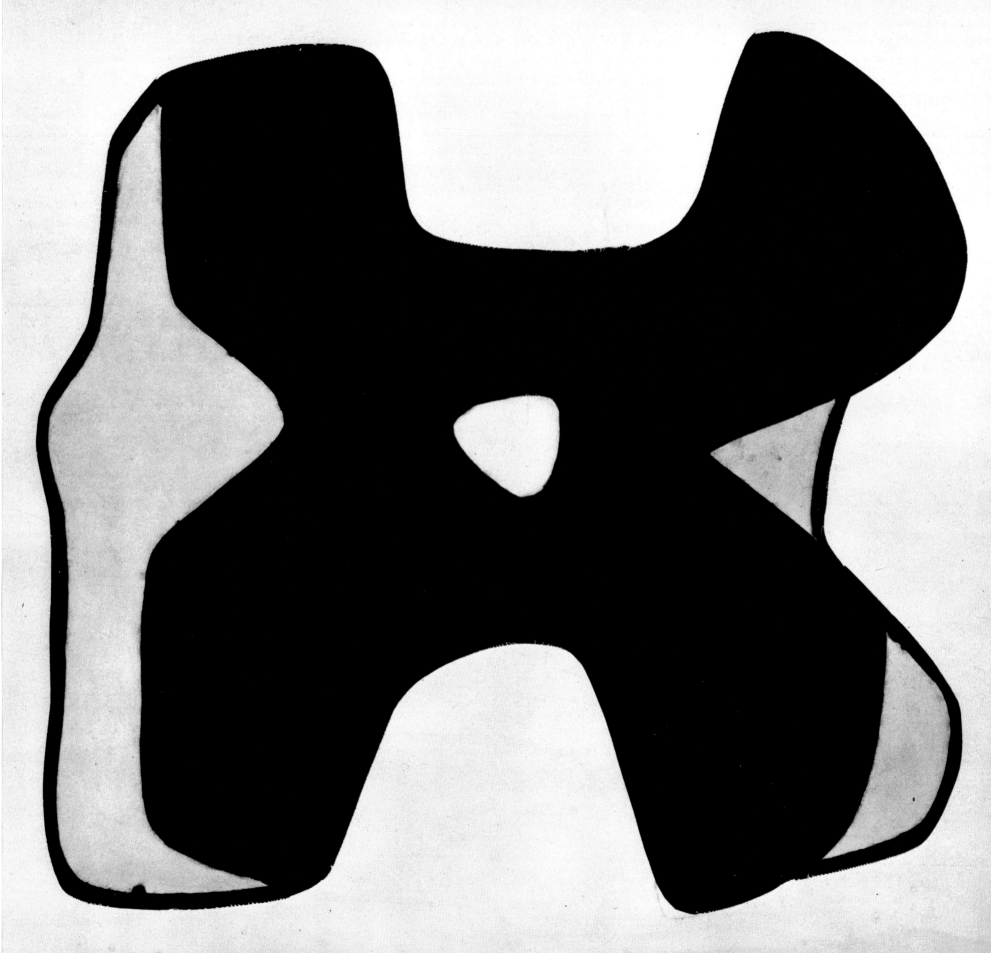

89. Drawing.

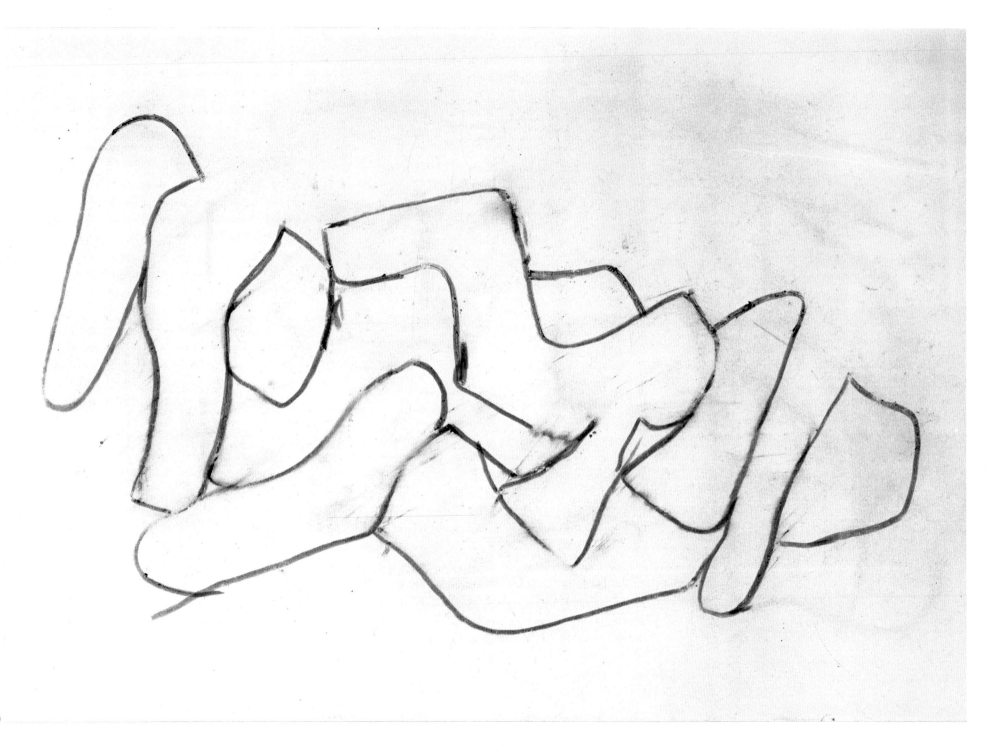

90. L-70. 1970. Canvas collage, 157 × 192 cm. Galerie Schmela Collection, Düsseldorf.

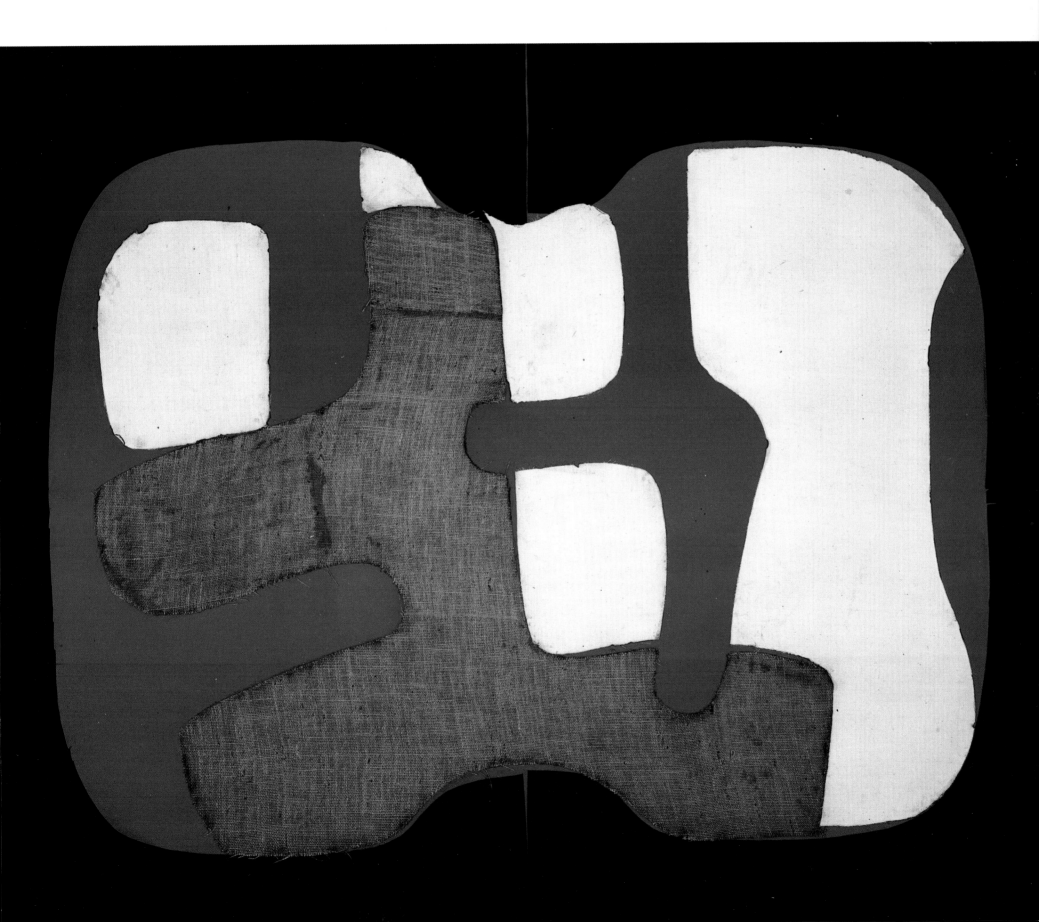

91

91. Drawing.

92. I-L-6-72. 1972. Canvas collage, 153 × 168 cm.

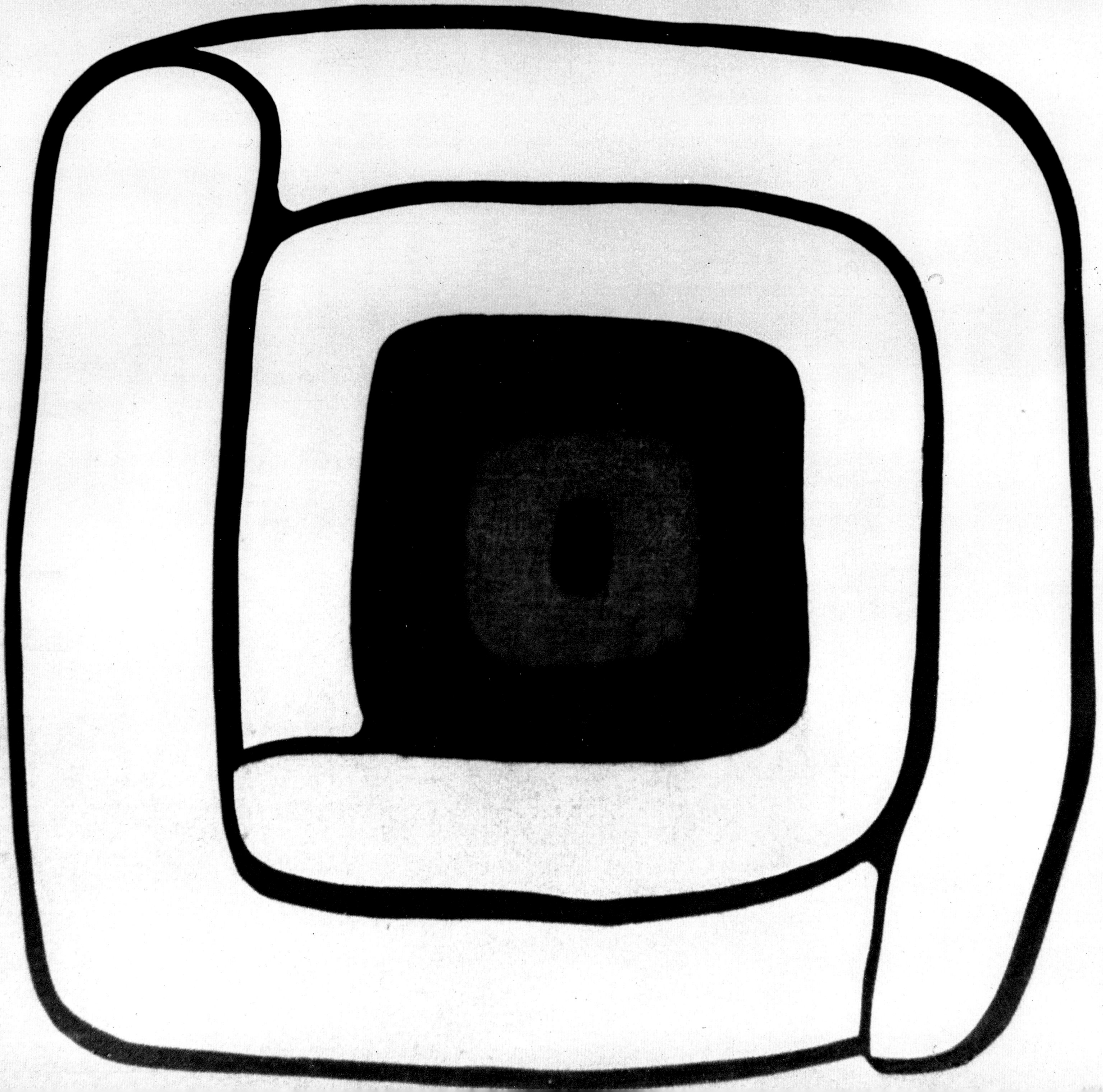

93. LL-2-72-A & B. B & C. 1972. Canvas collage, 240 × 164 cm.

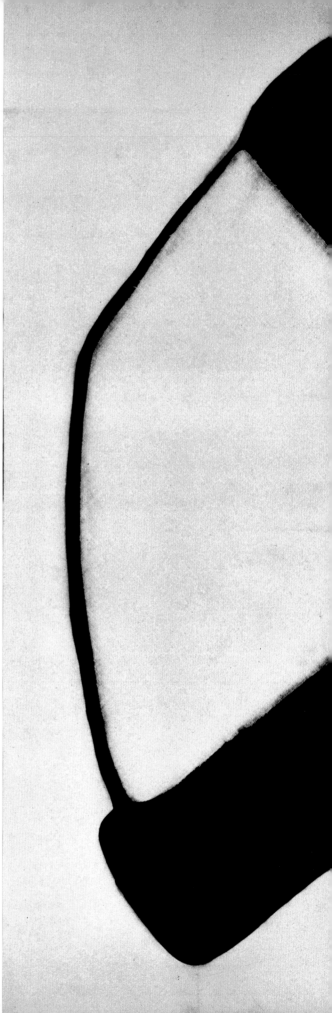

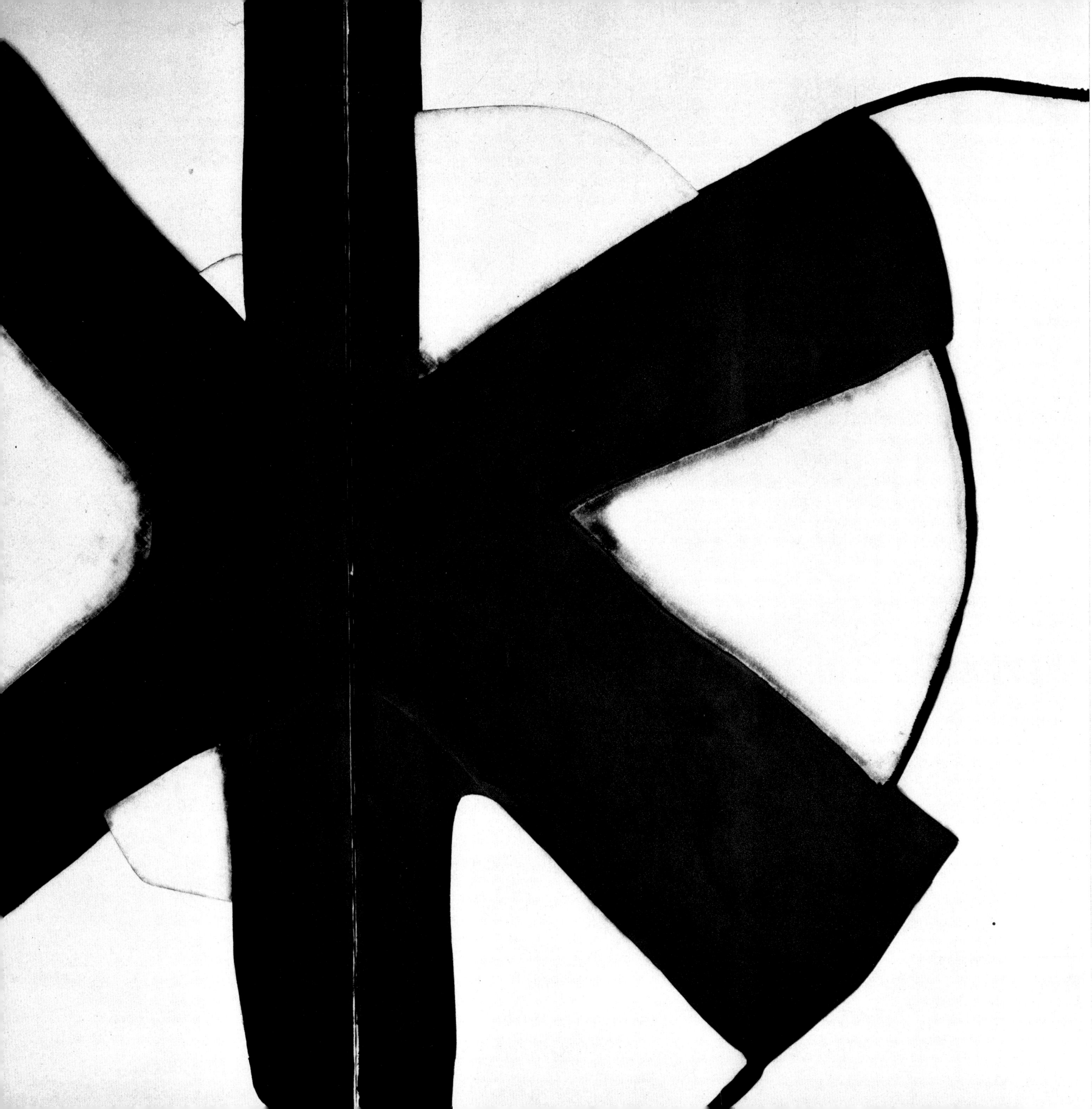

94. M-9-71. 1971. Oil and canvas collage, 81.3 × 91.5 cm.

95. S-6-73. 1973. Canvas collage, 50 × 65 cm.

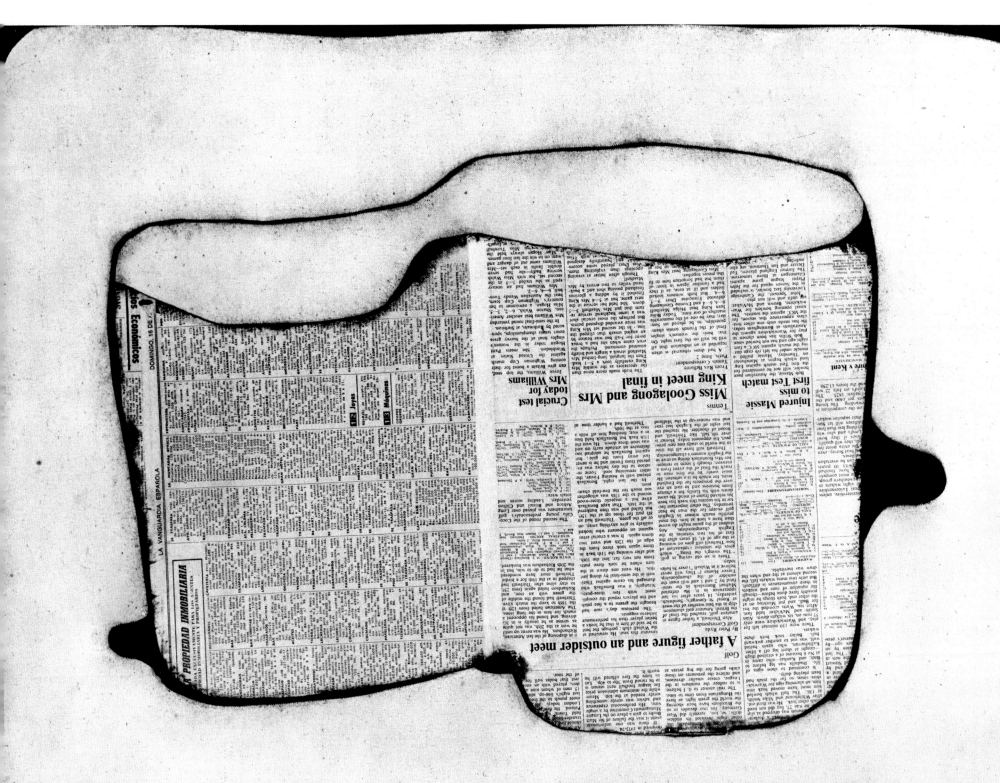

95

96. Drawing.
97. M-12-71. 1971. Canvas collage, 91.5 × 81 cm.

96

97

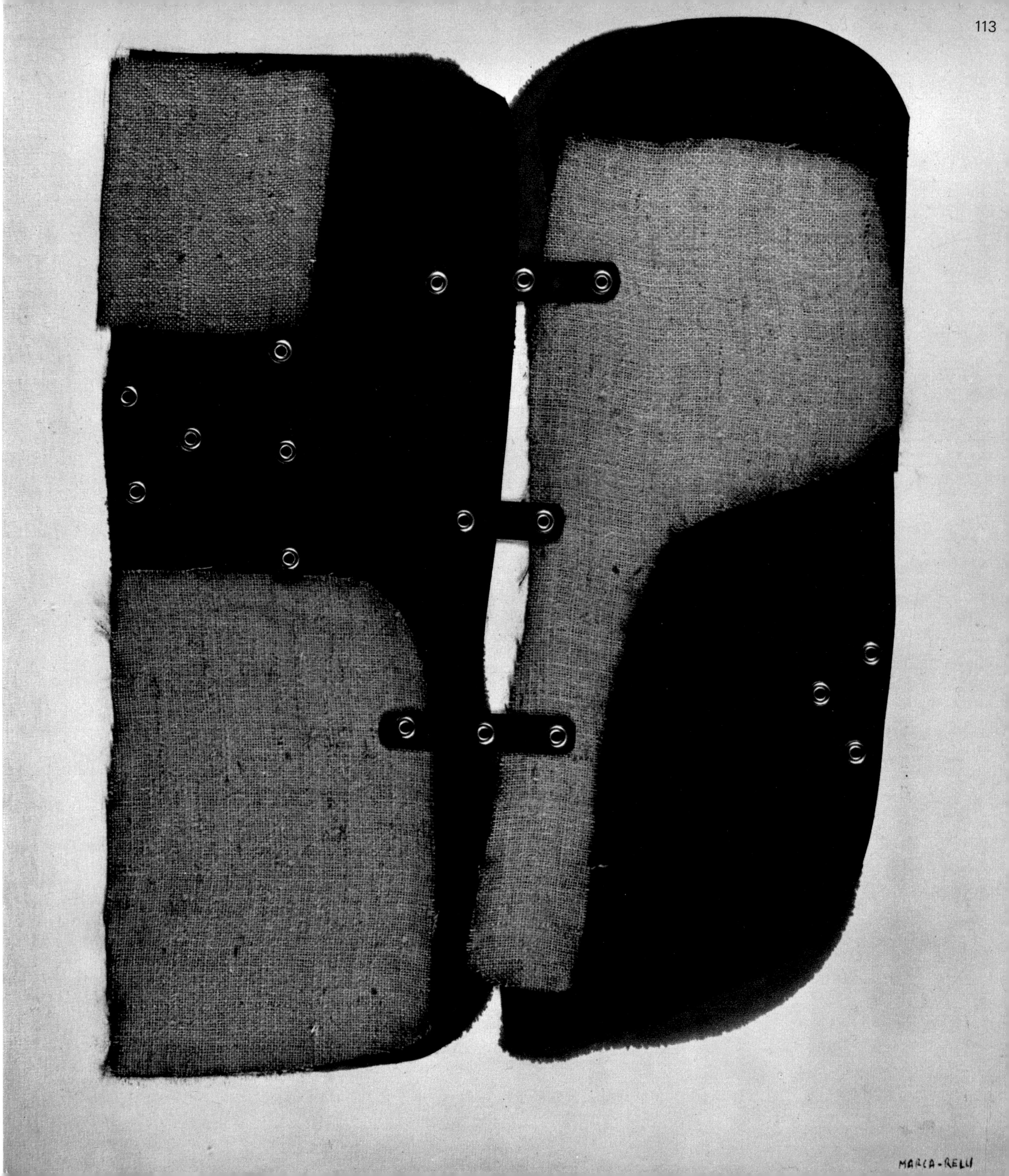

98. Figure (S-3-65). 1965. Canvas collage, 55.5 × 48 cm.

99. Reclining Figure (X5-20-68). 1968. Painted canvas collage, 55.5 × 61 cm.

98

100. Figure (Y-M-8-70). 1970. Collage, 63.5 × 86 cm.

101. L-1-71. 1971. Painted canvas collage, 167.5 × 167.5 cm.

100

102. XM-20-71. 1971. Canvas collage, 81 × 91.5 cm.

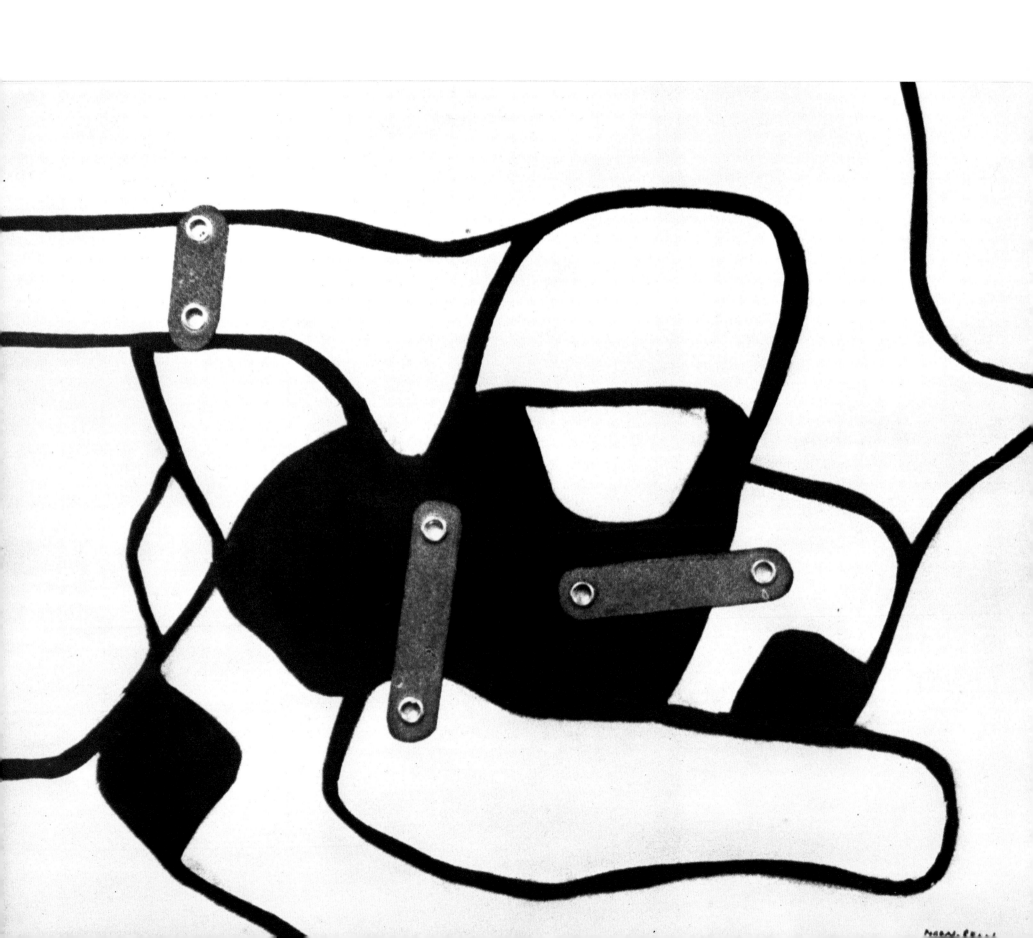

103. Drawing.

104. Drawing.

105. L-5-66. 1966. Canvas collage, 122 × 167.5 cm.

104

106. Multiple image (L-14-69). 1969. Mixed media collage on canvas, 145 × 176.5 cm.

107. Untitled (S-1-69). 1969. Canvas collage, 61 × 56 cm.

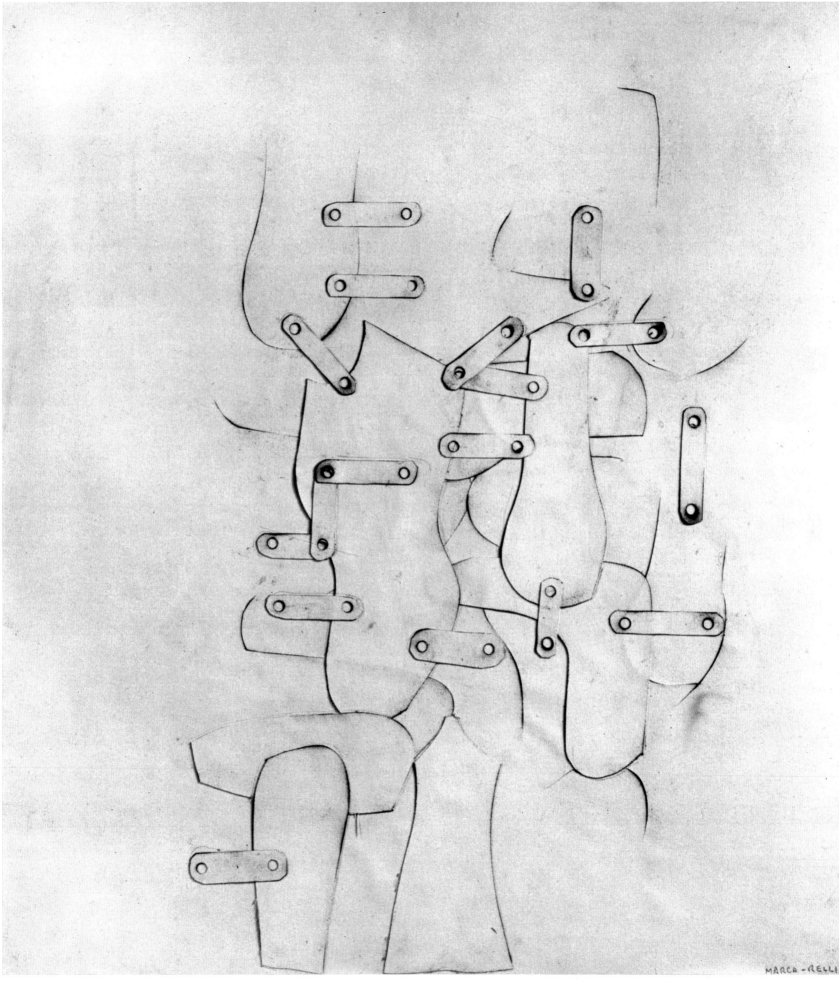

MARCA-RELLI

108. Figure-Form I (M-1-66). 1966. Painted canvas collage, 89 × 114 cm.
109. Drawing.

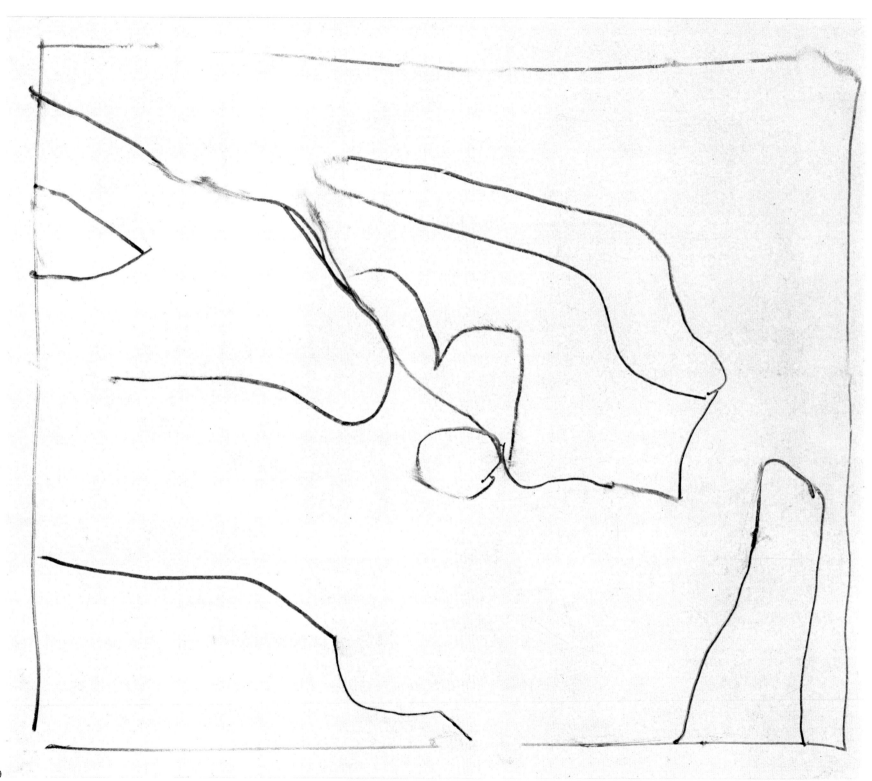

109

110. Drawing.

111. Torso (L-1-69). 1969. Mixed media collage on canvas, 145.5 × 176.5 cm.
Private collection.

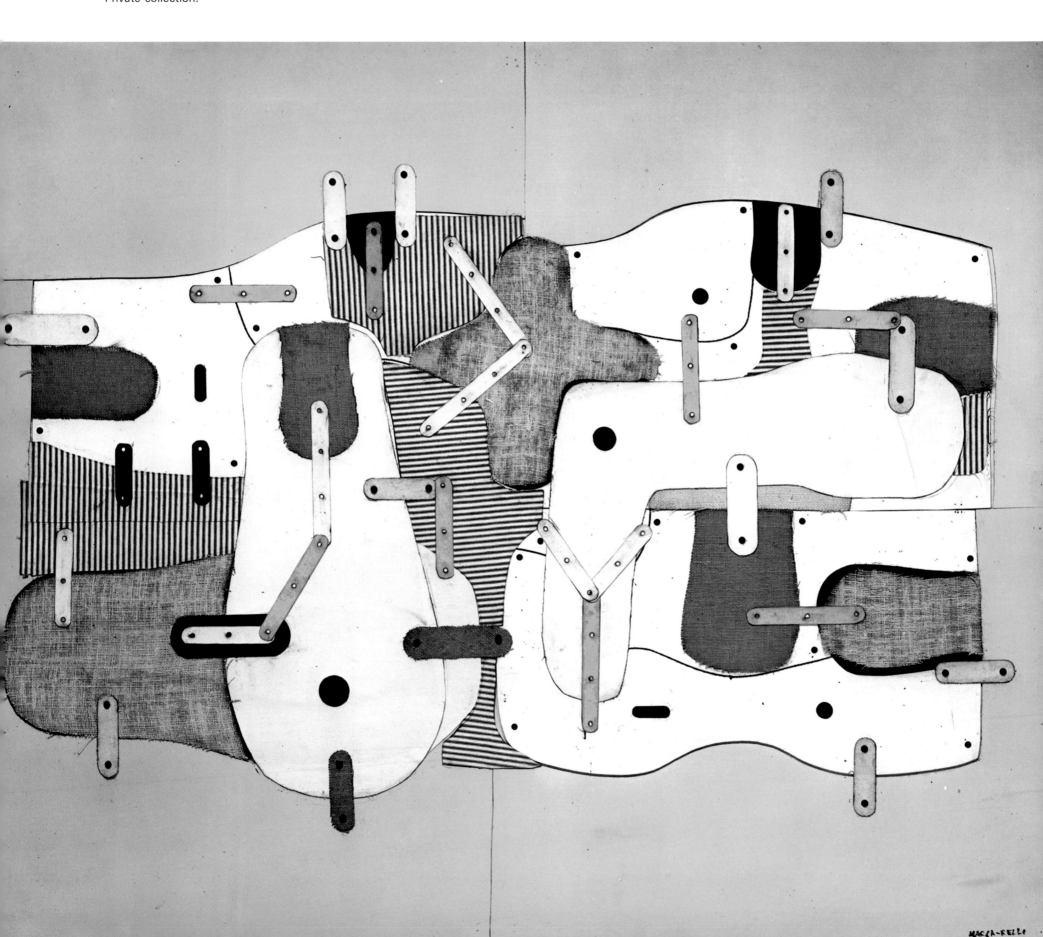

112. Reclining figure (F-L-6-67). 1967. Painted canvas collage, 144.5 × 176.5 cm.

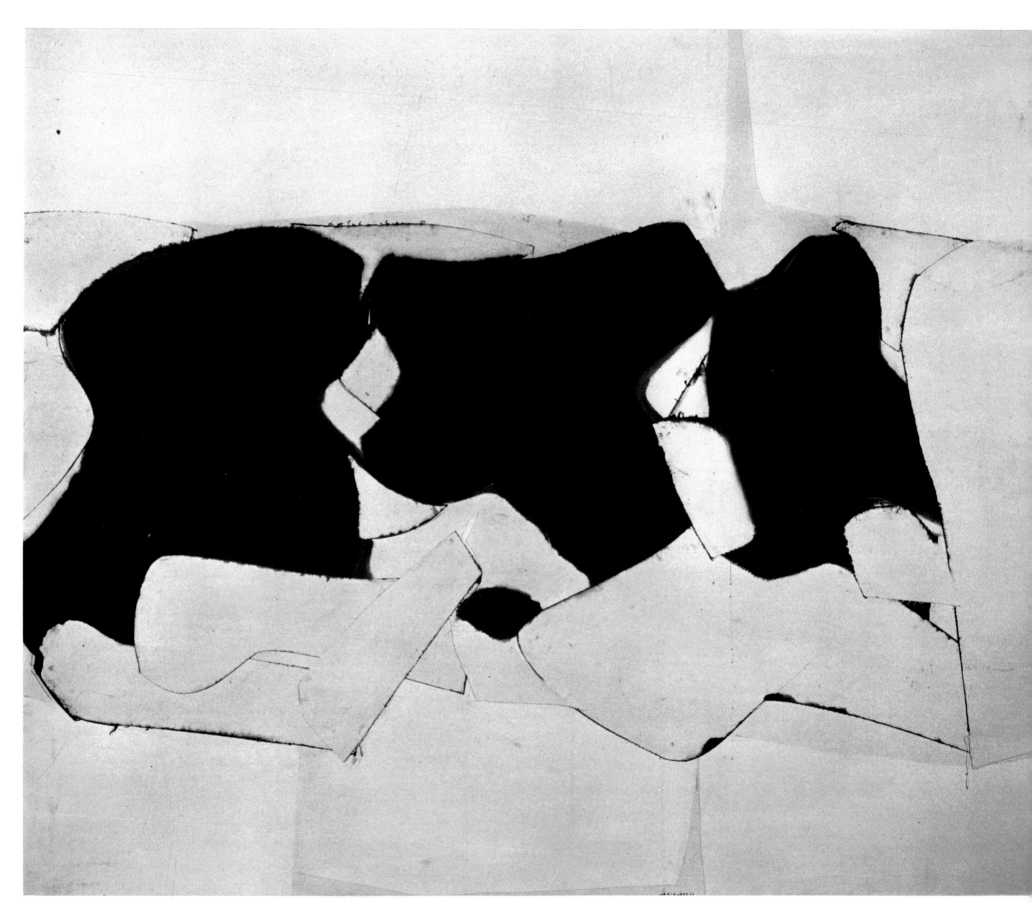

113. Drawing.

113

114. M-3-72. 1972. Canvas collage, 81 × 86 cm.

115. M-11-71. 1971. Oil and canvas collage, 32 × 36 cm.

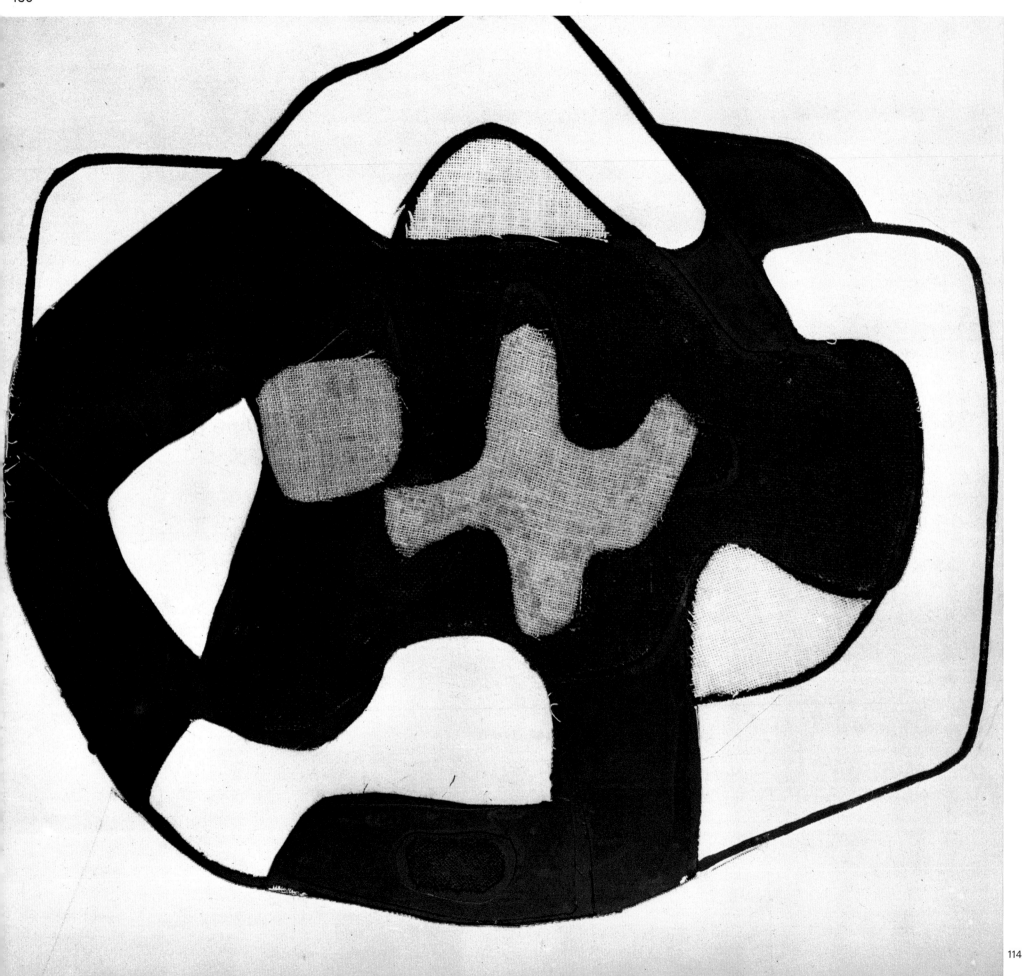

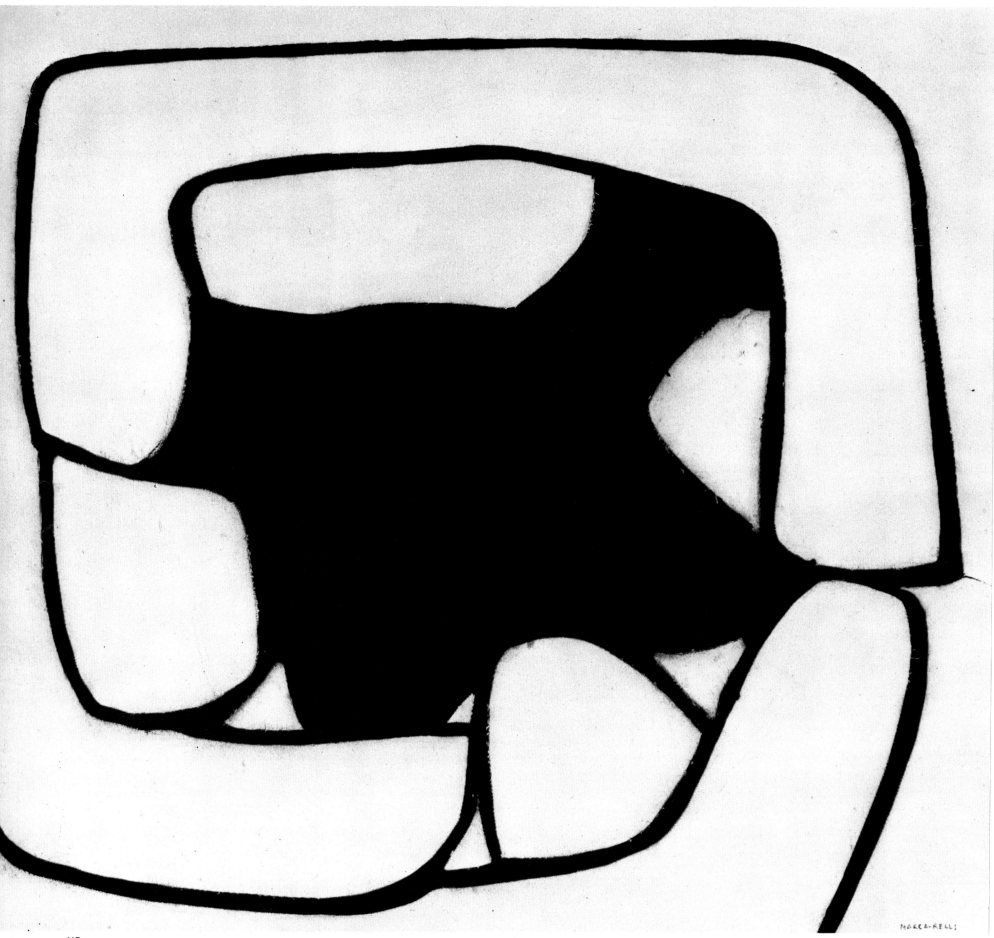

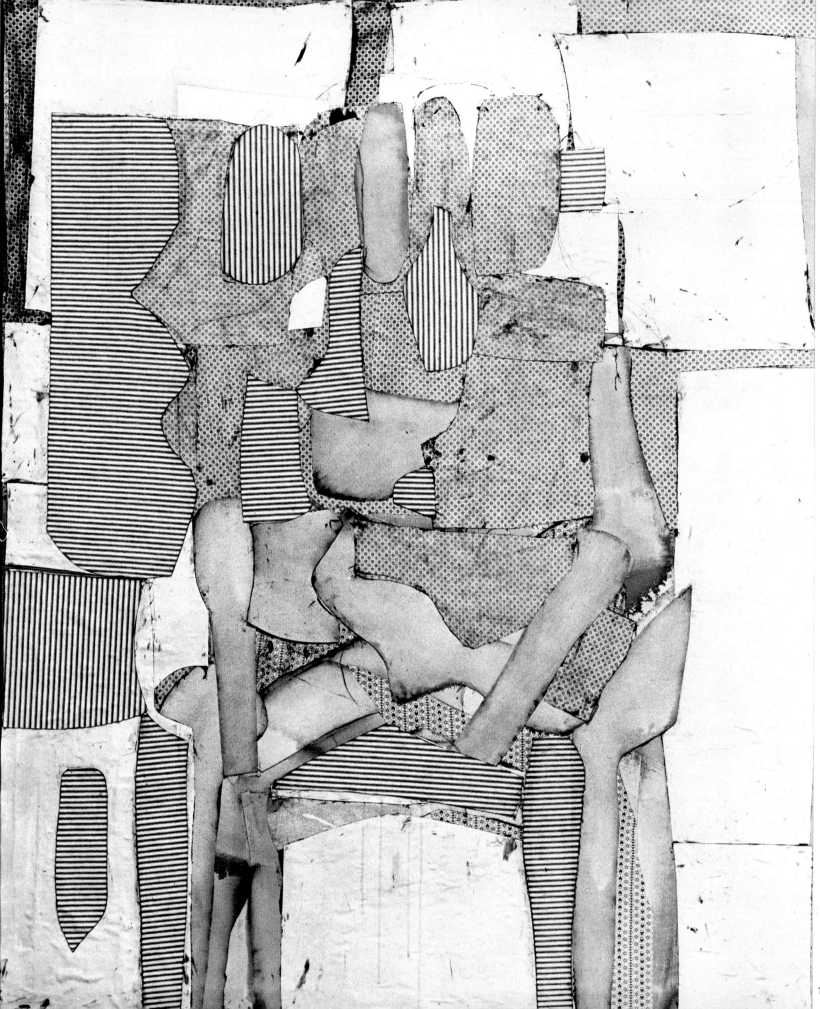

116. Figure (X-L-2-70-71).
1970-1971. Canvas collage, 177 × 144 cm.

117. X-M-4-70. 1970. Canvas collage, 81 × 91.5 cm.

118. X-M-7-70. 1970. Canvas collage, 81 × 91.5 cm.

119. M-6-71. 1971. Canvas collage, 81 × 91.5 cm.

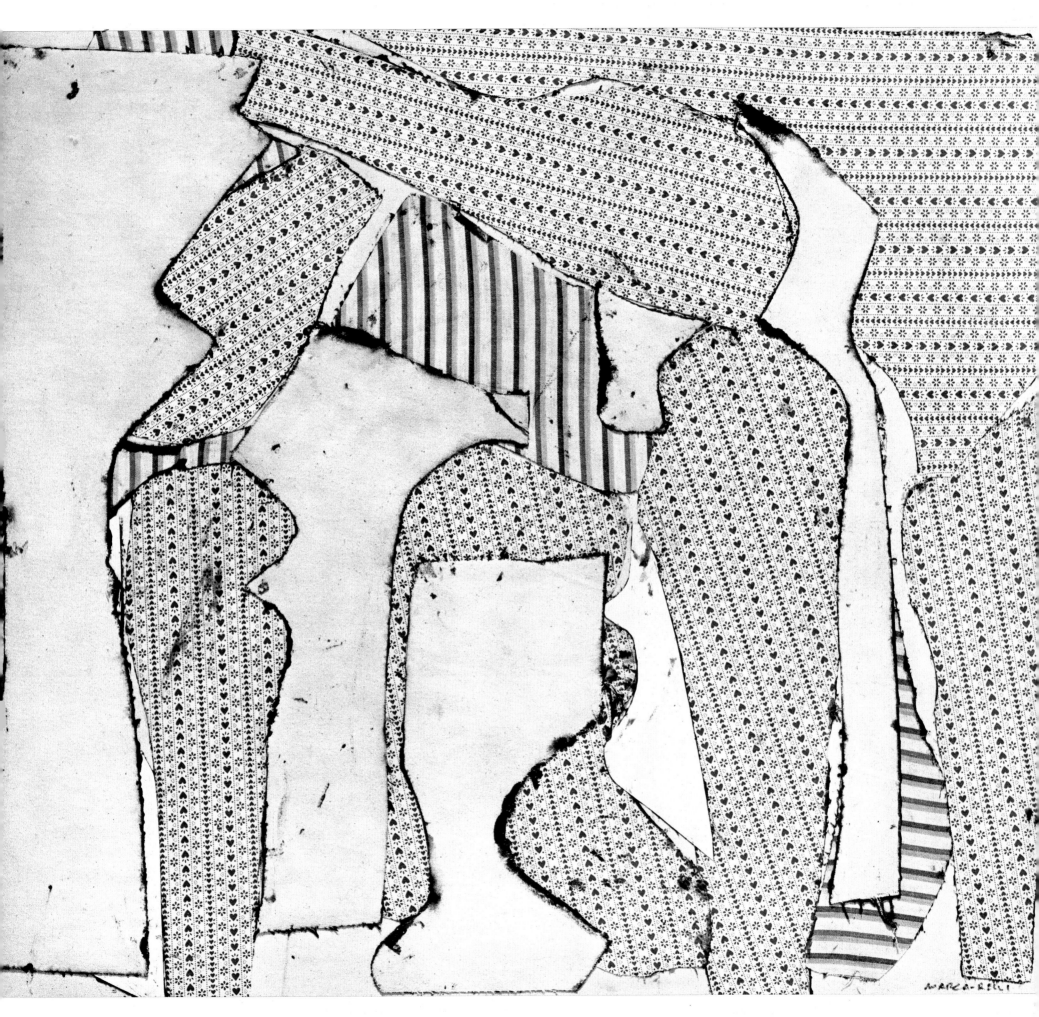

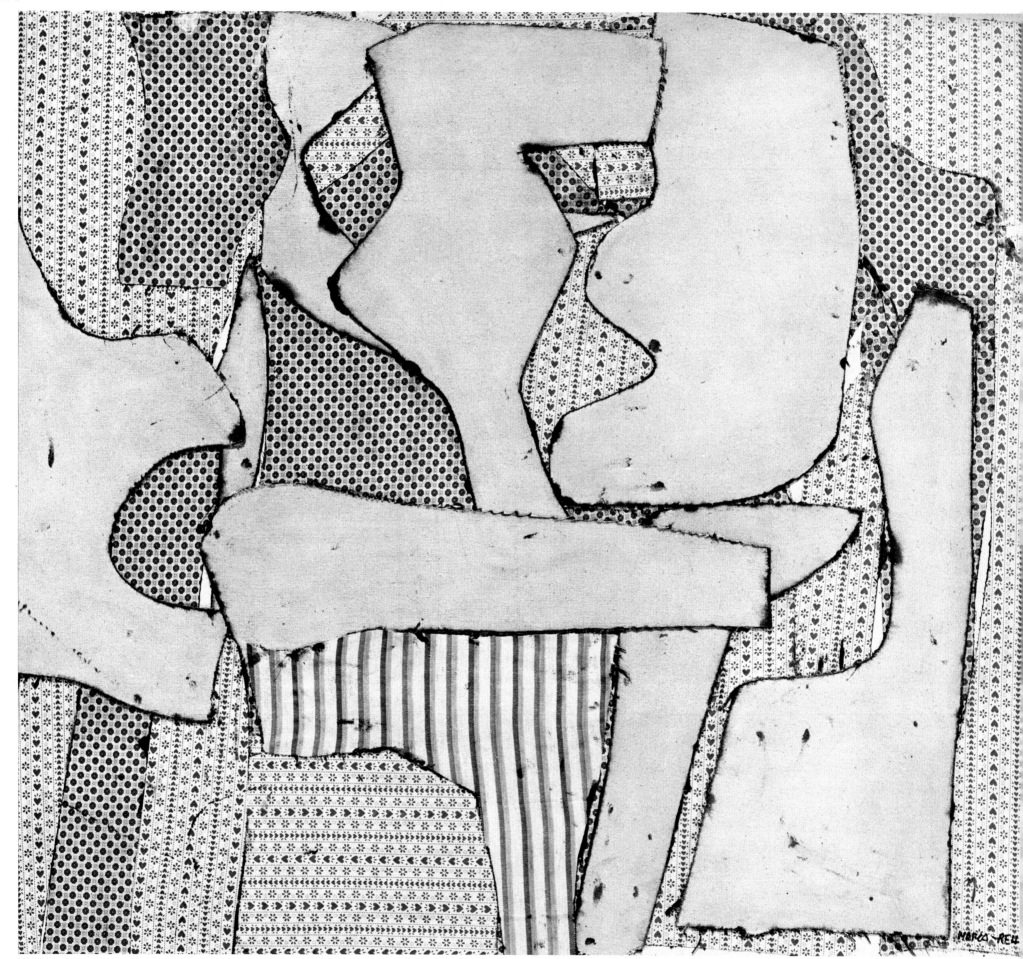

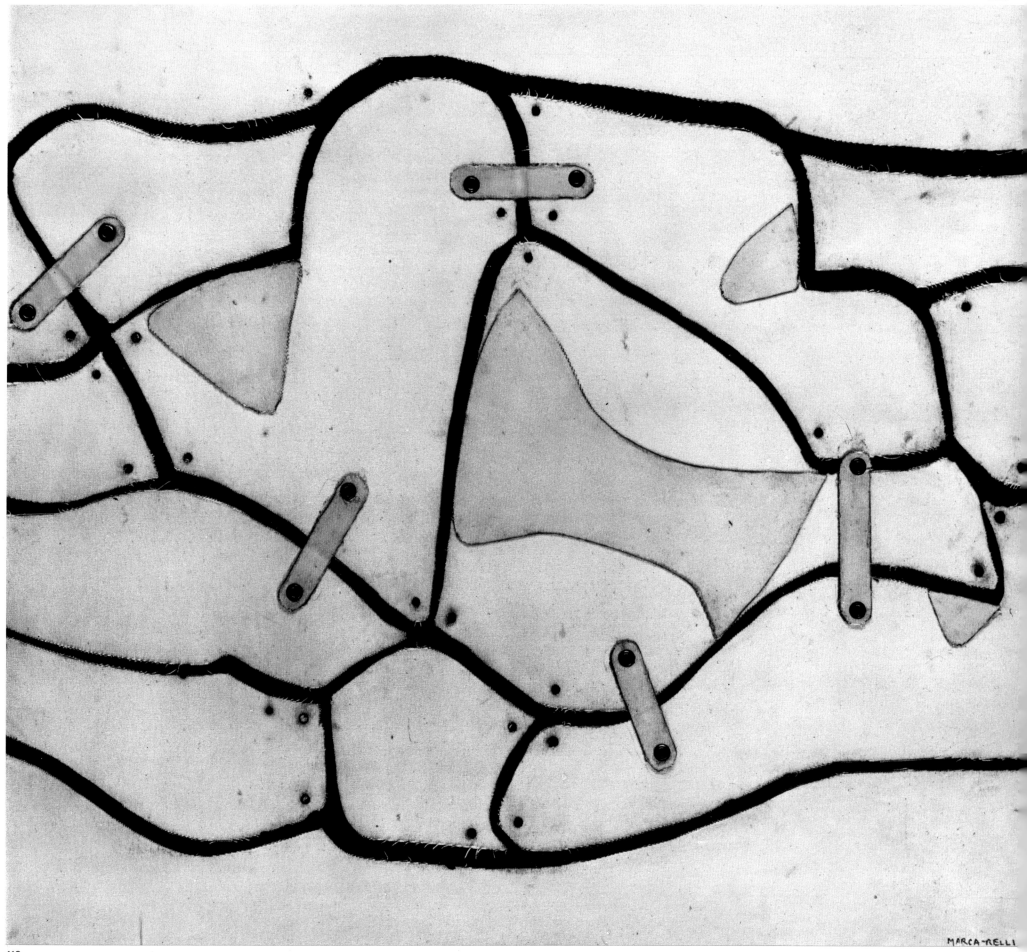

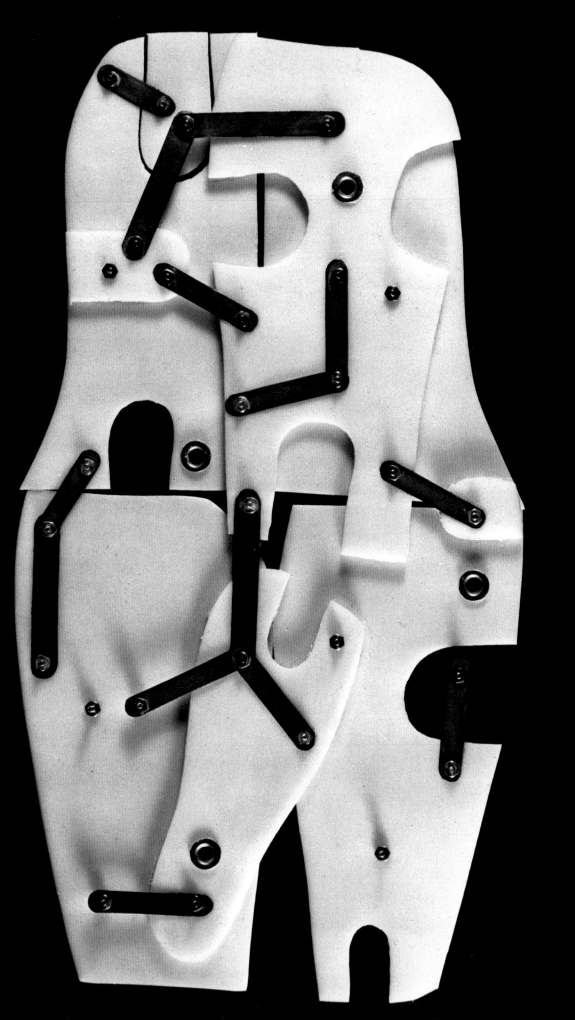

120. Untitled relief No. 6 (R-SCP-6-69). 1969. Mixed media, 56 × 36 cm.

121. M-13-71. 1971. Canvas collage, 81 × 91.5 cm.

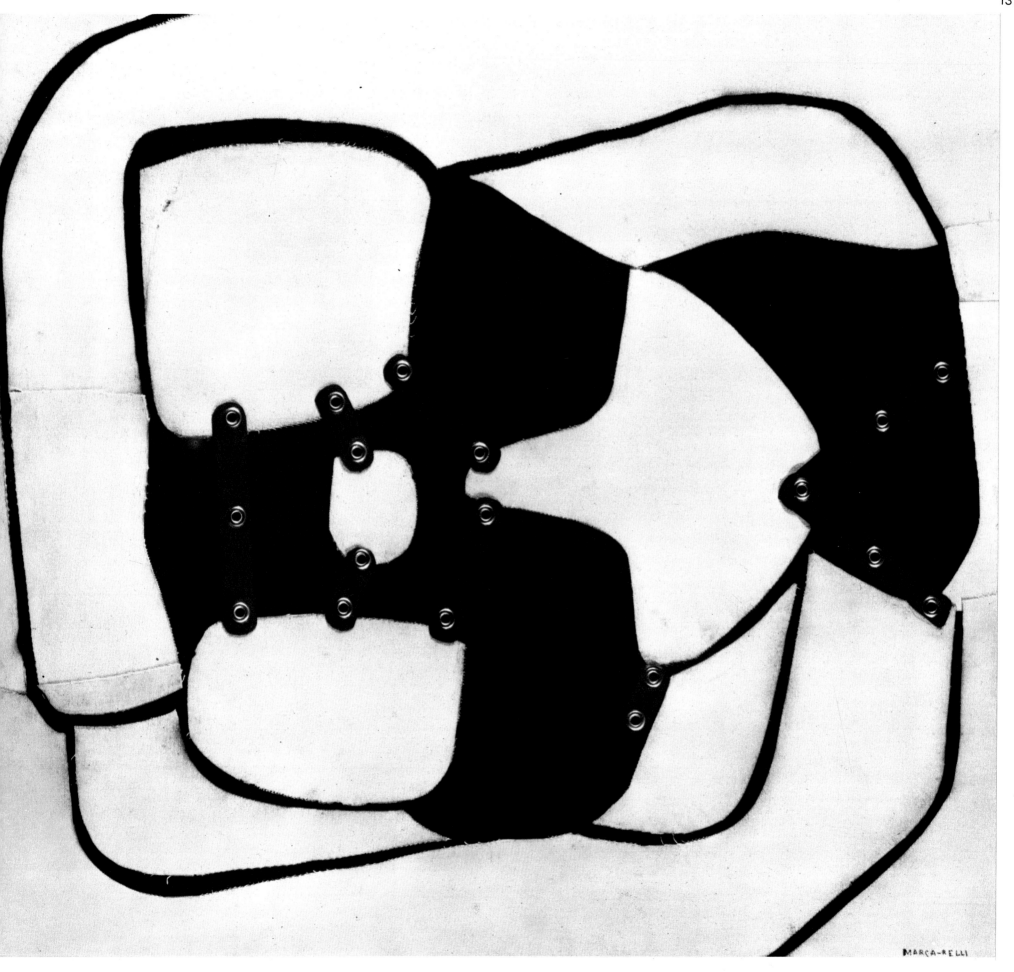

122. LL-2-71. A & B. 1971. Painted canvas collage, 228 × 168 cm.

123. M-8-71. 1971. Canvas collage, 81 × 91.5 cm.

124. M-10-71. 1971. Canvas collage, 81 × 91.5 cm.

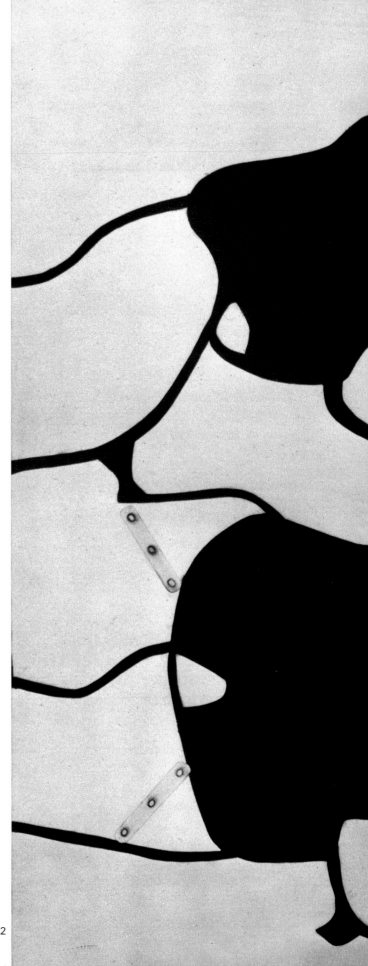

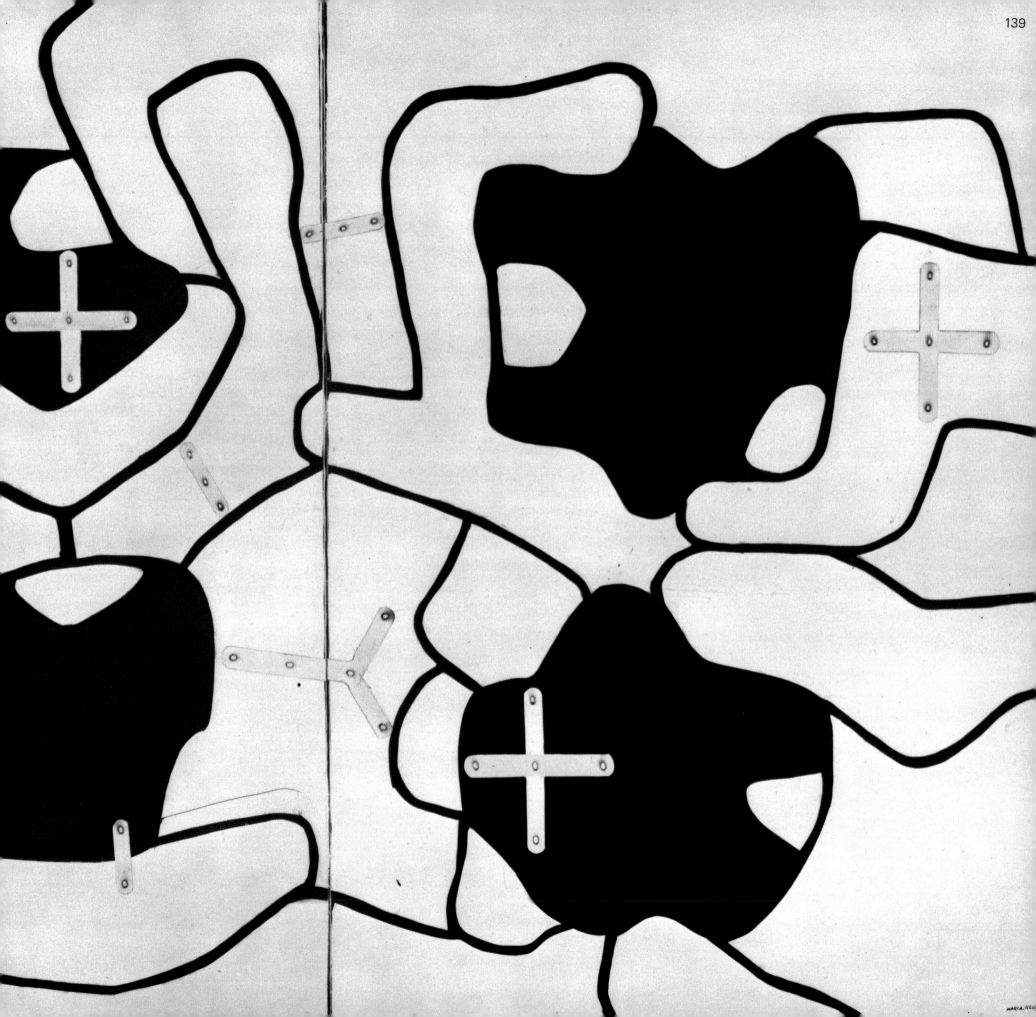

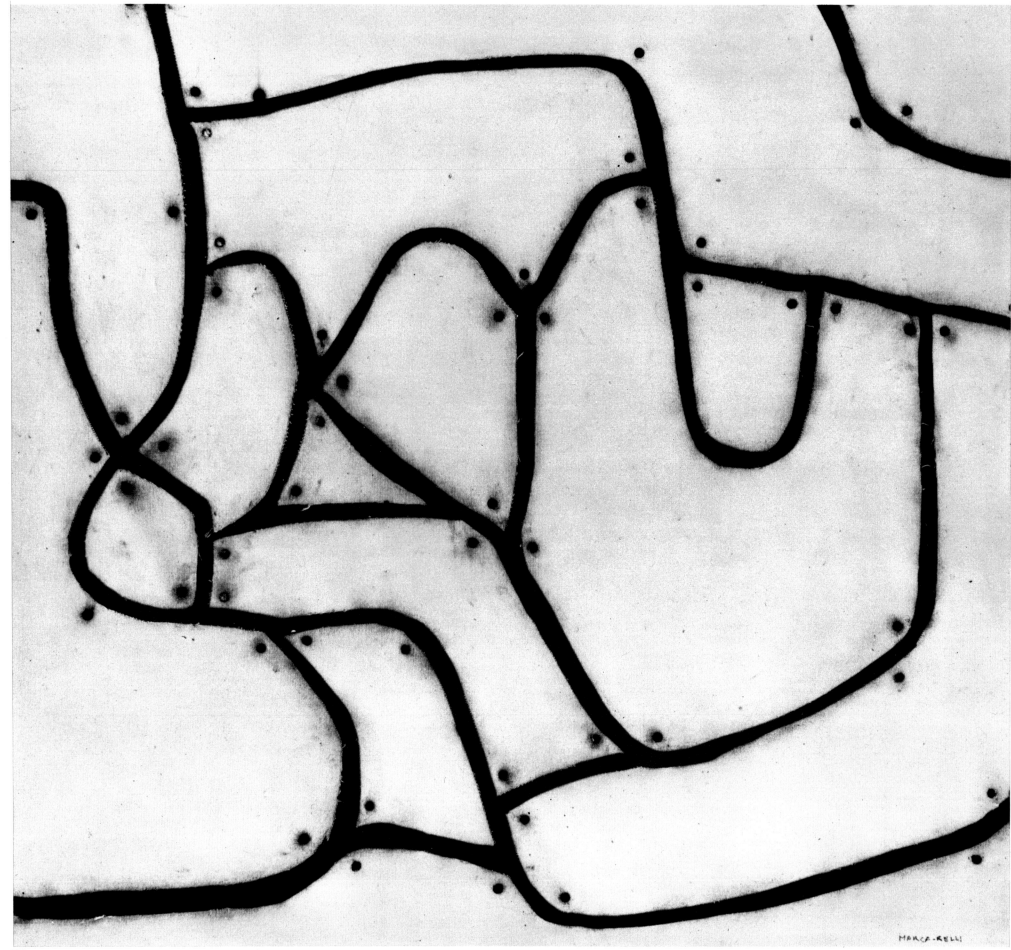

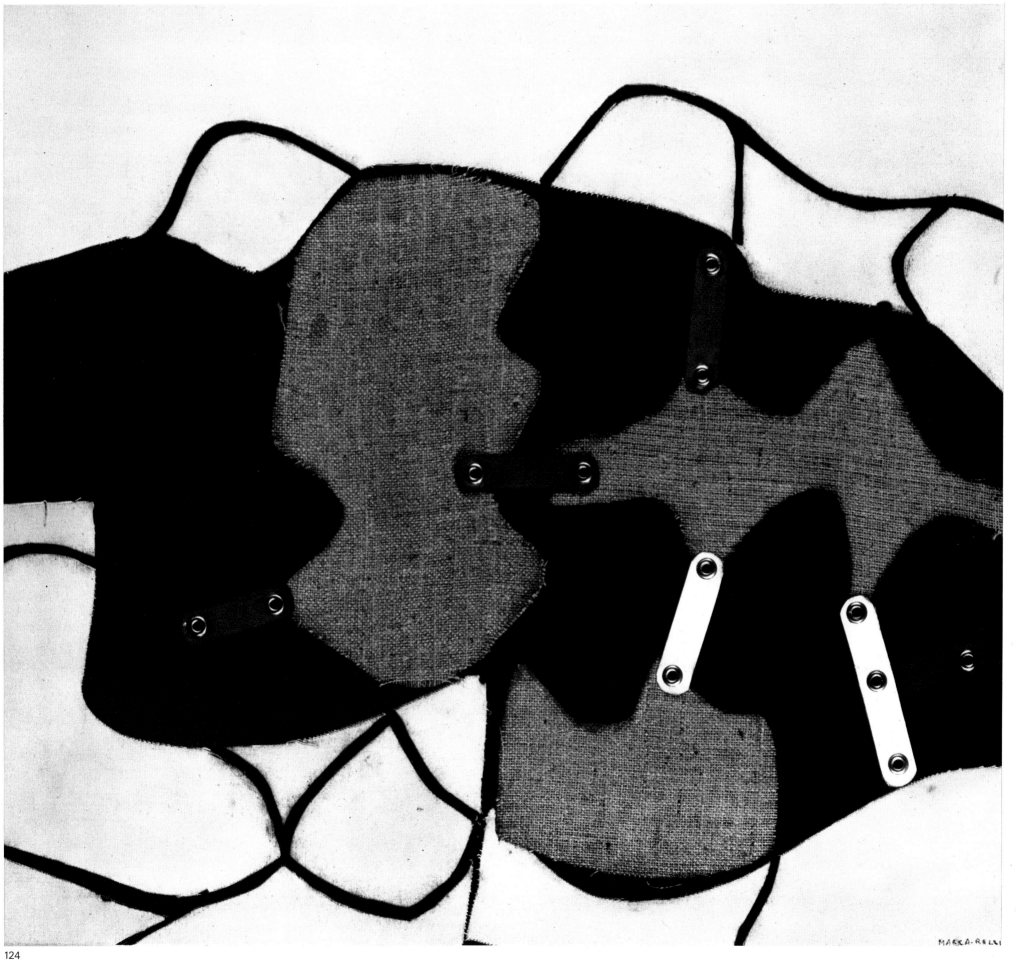

125. Drawing.

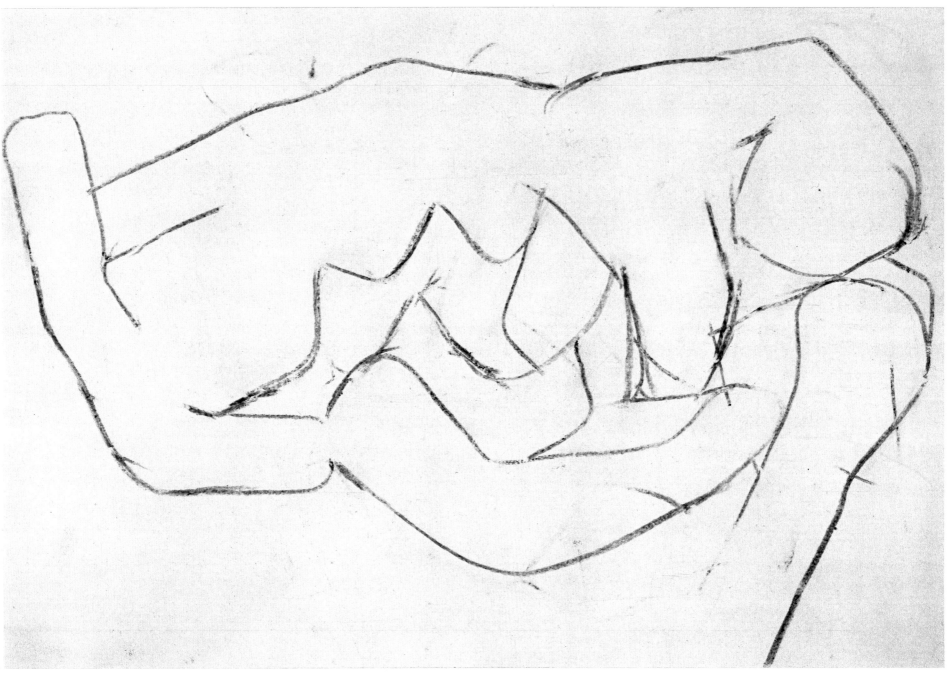

126.   S-3-73. 1973. Newspaper collage, 53 × 65 cm.

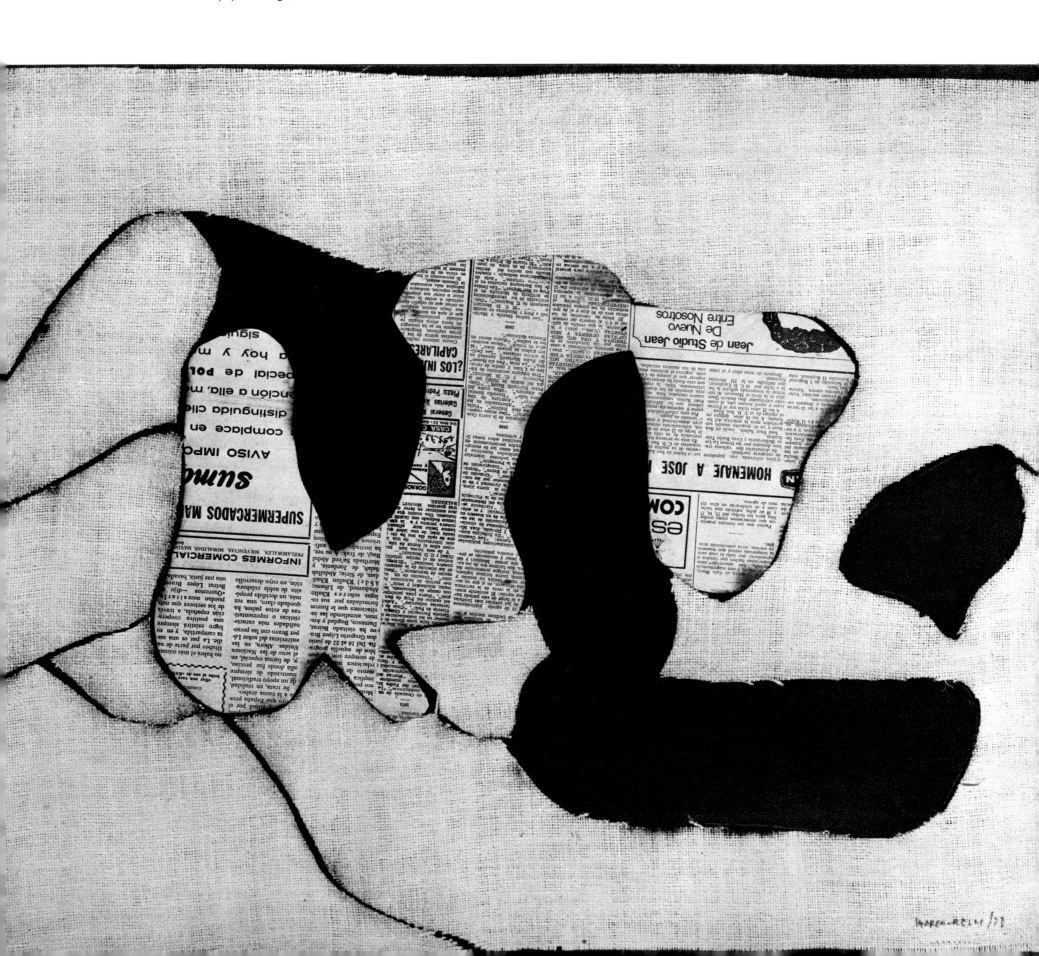

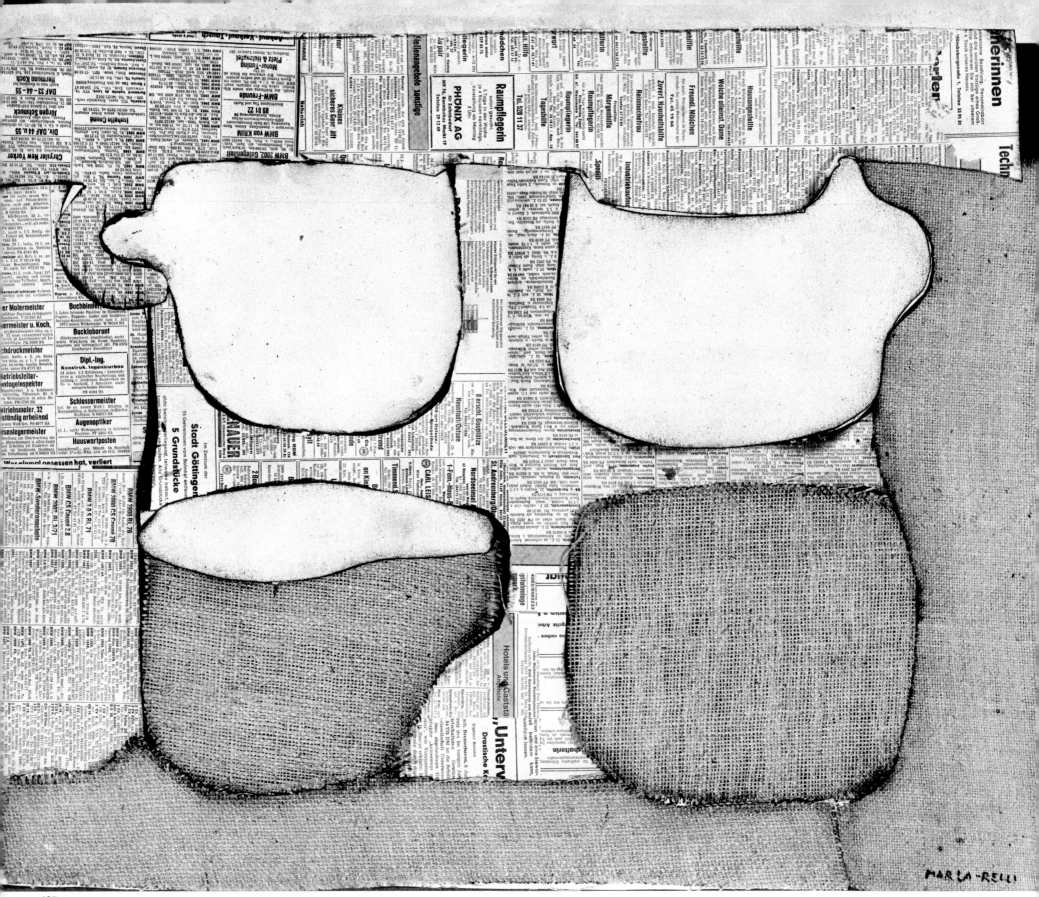

127. Cupsy (S-15-72). 1972.
Newspaper collage, 52
× 65 cm.

128. Figure (S-9-73). 1973.
Newspaper collage, 66
× 50 cm.

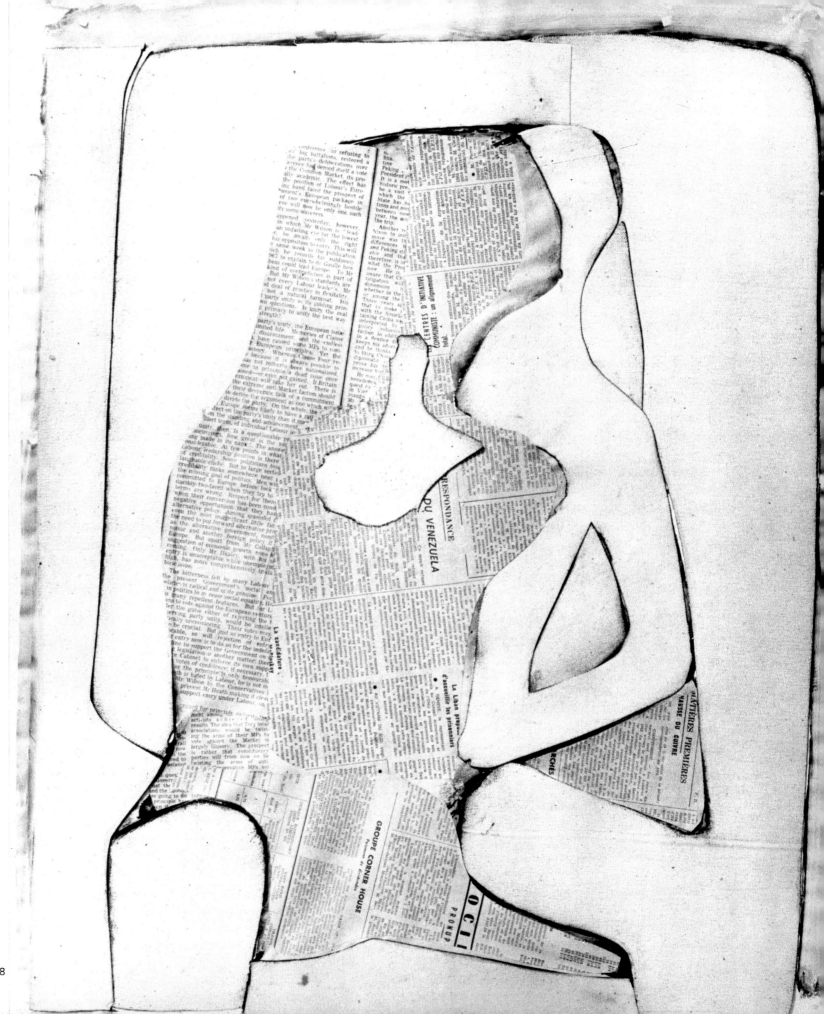

128

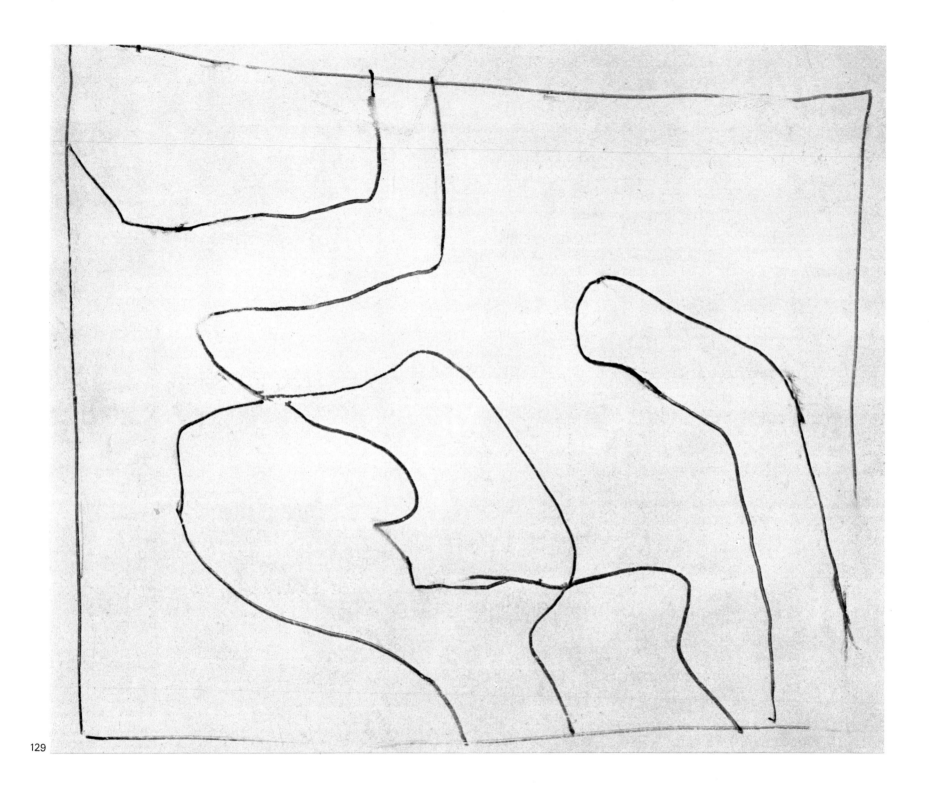

129

129. Drawing.

130. Figure (OS-20-73). 1973. Collage, 53 × 71 cm.

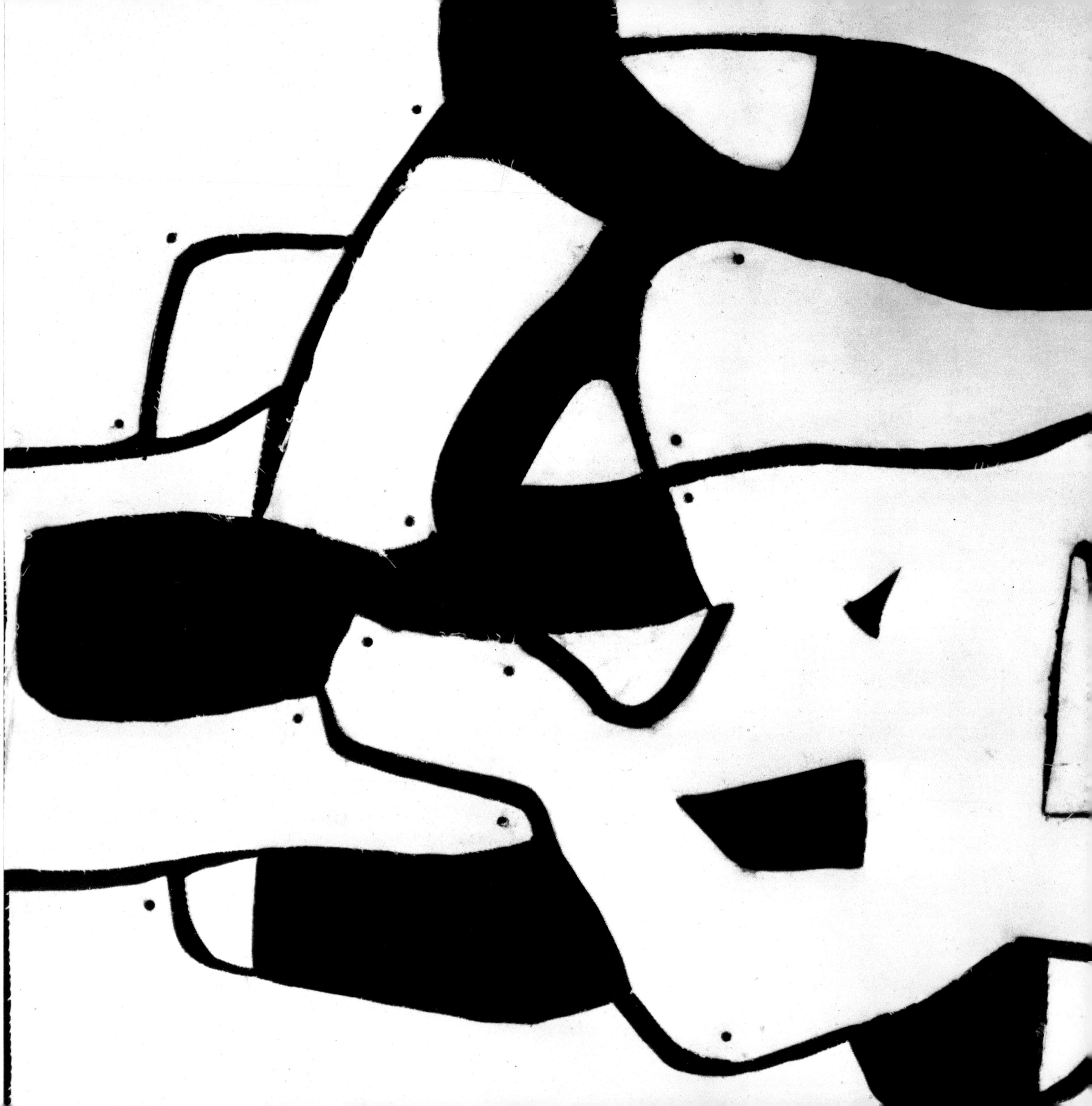

131

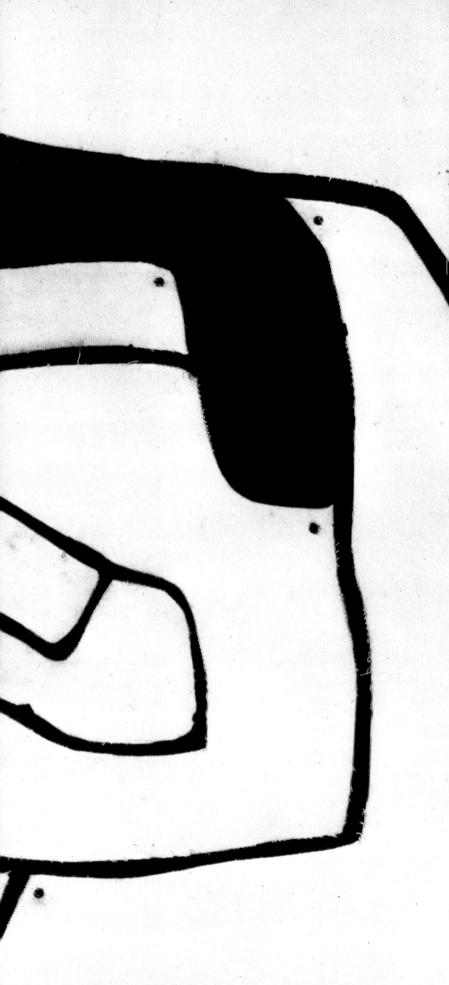

131. Figures (M-14-71). 1971. Canvas collage, 81.3 × 122 cm.

132. Drawing.

133. M-1-73. 1973. Canvas and newspaper collage, 99 × 159 cm.

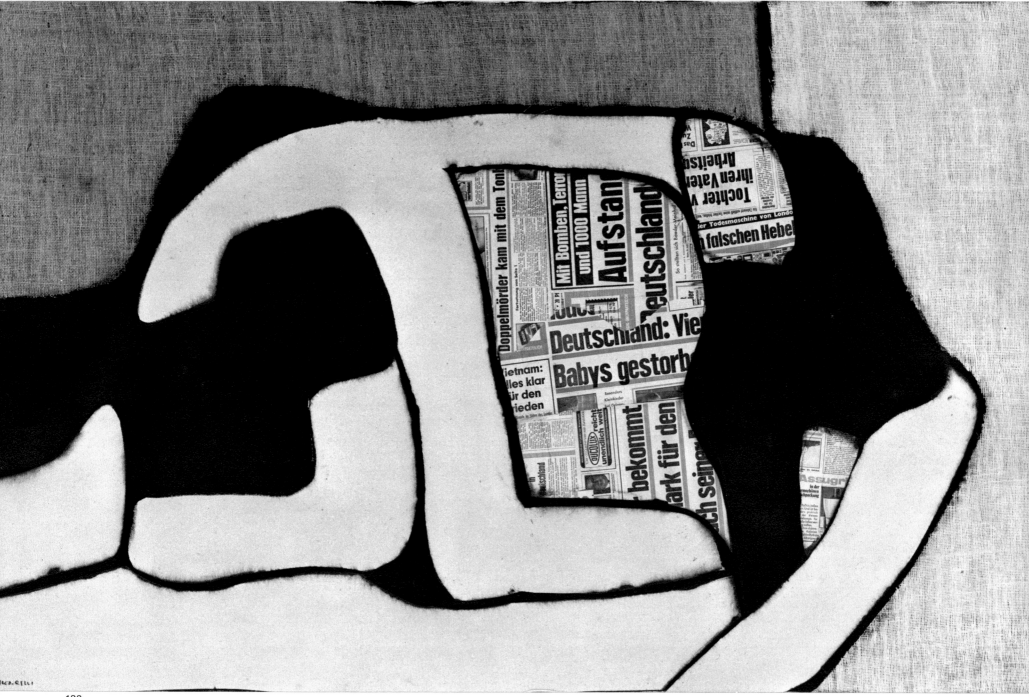

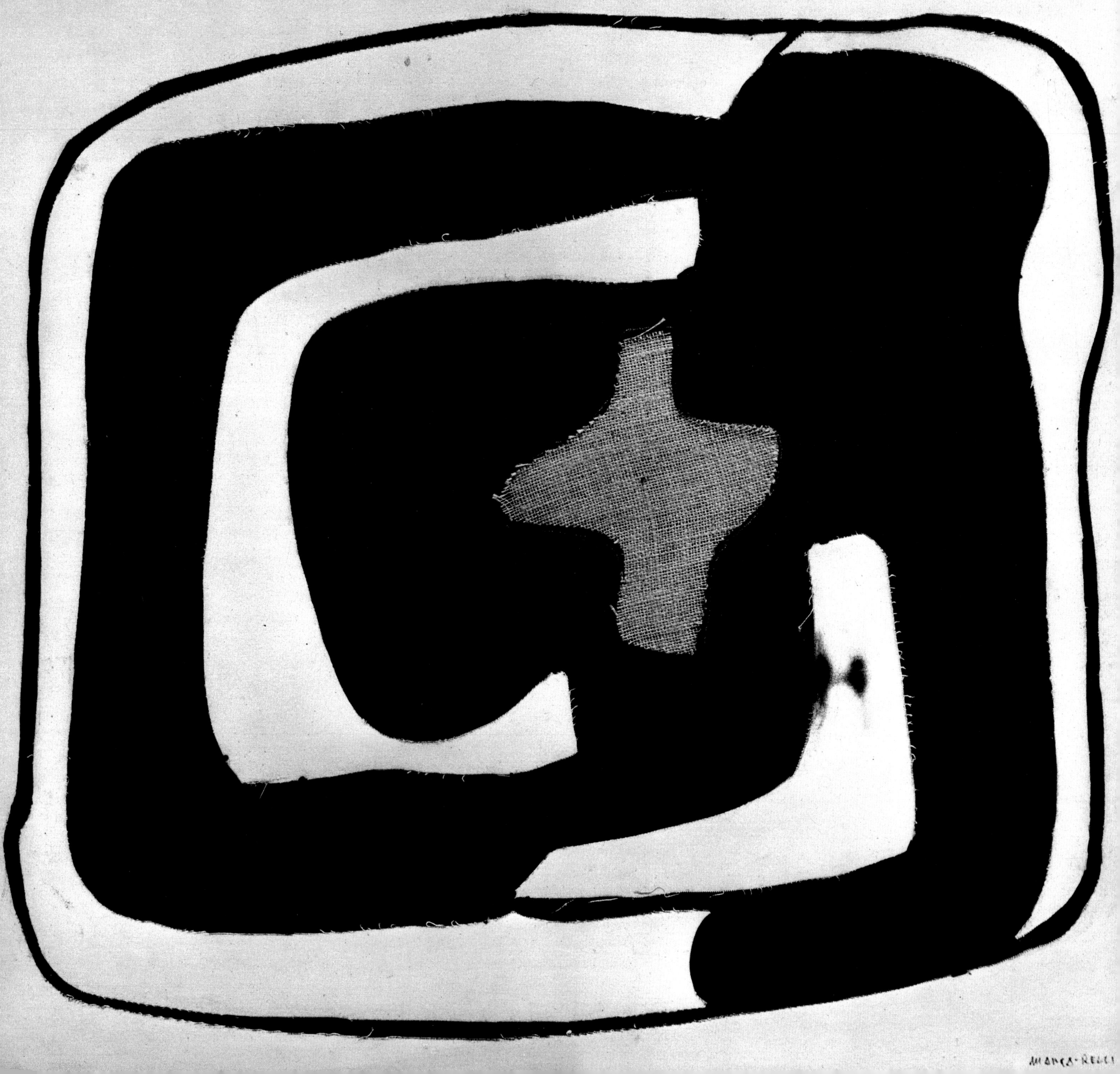
MARCA-RELLI

134. Y-M-15-71. 1971. Canvas collage, 81.3 × 175.8 cm.

135. Figure (M-9-73). 1973. Canvas collage, 94 × 116 cm.

135

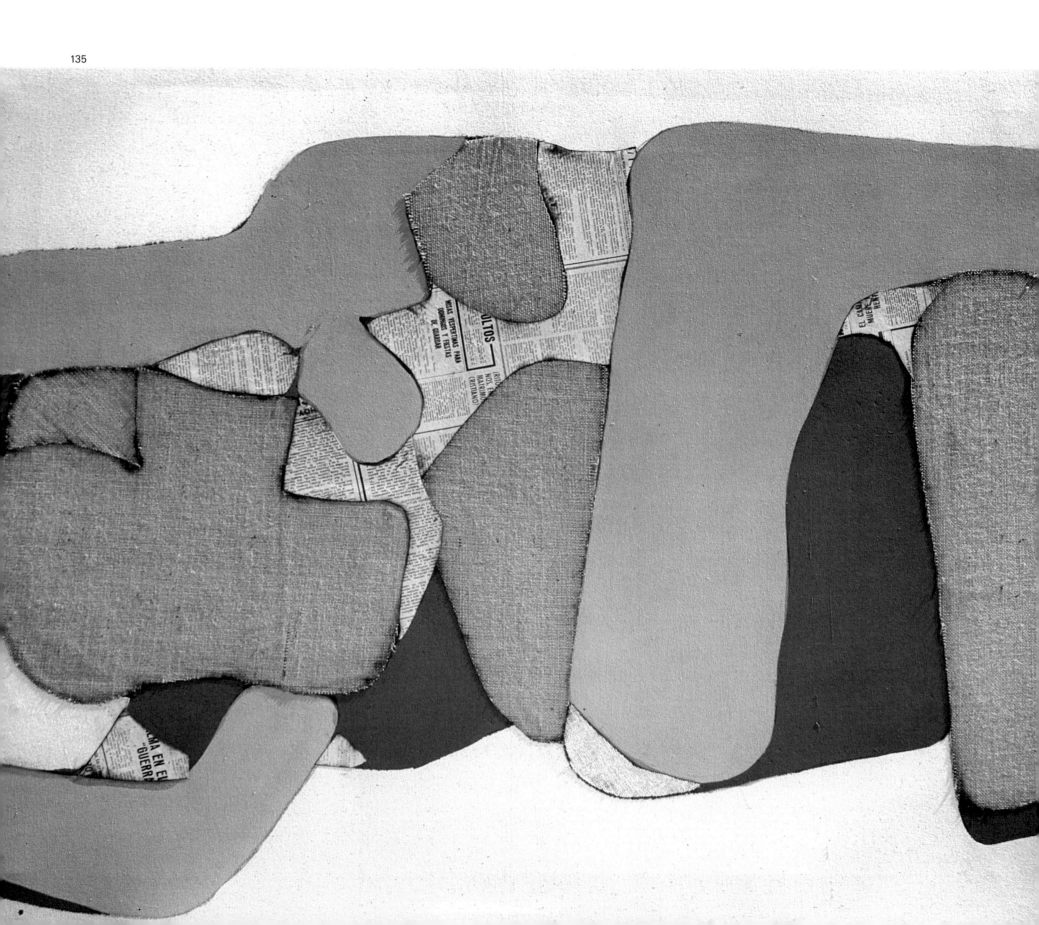

136. Drawing.

137. M-3-73. 1973. Canvas and newspaper collage, 99 × 159 cm.

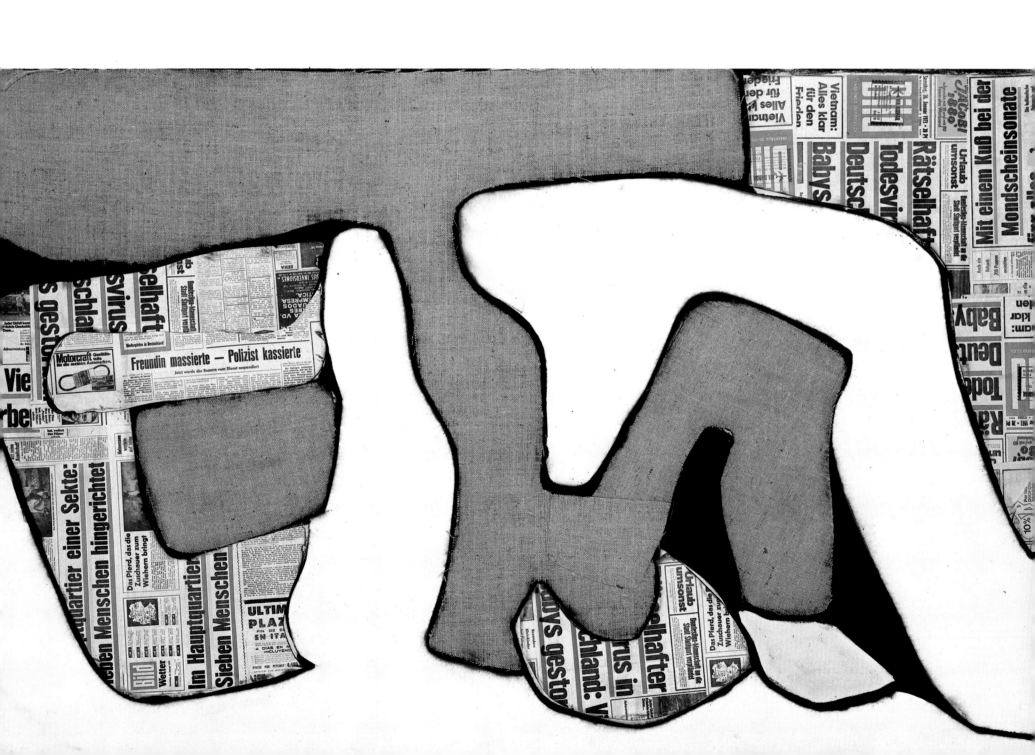

138. S-4-72. 1972. Newspaper collage, 51 × 65 cm. Private collection.

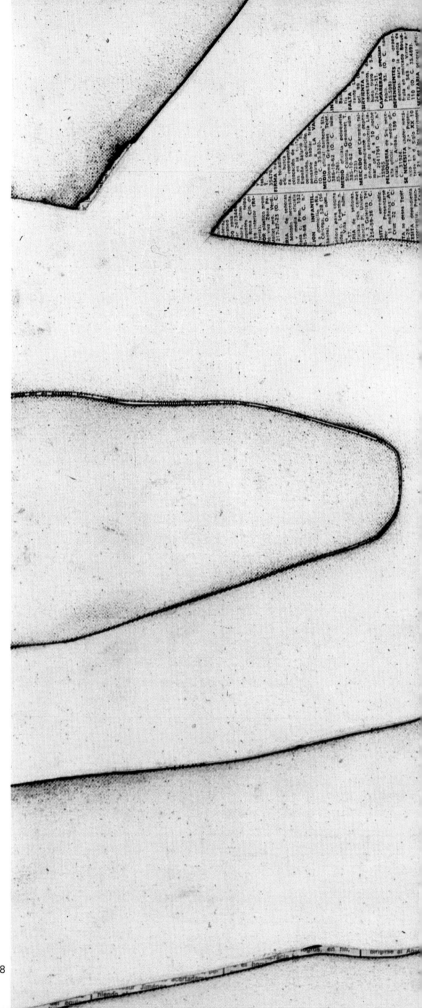

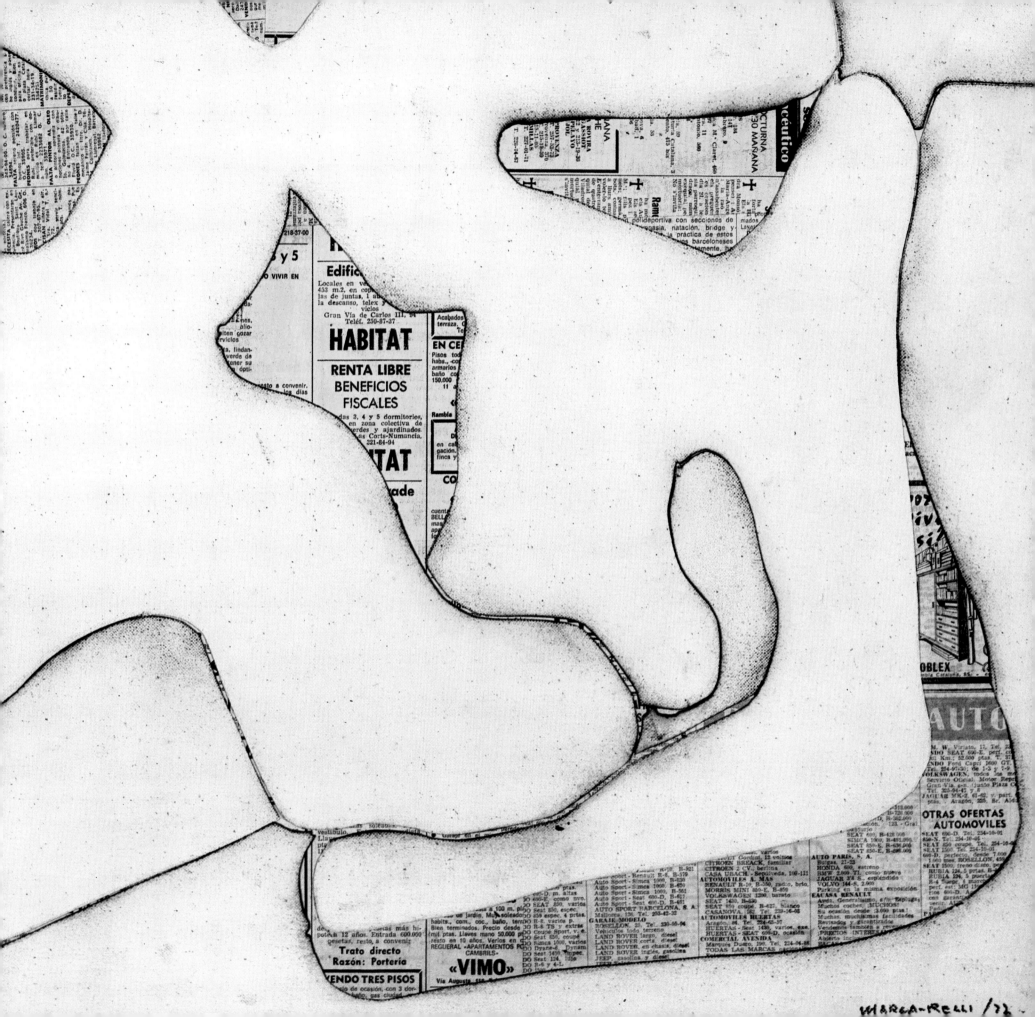

139. S-2-73. 1973. Canvas collage, 99 × 159 cm.

139

140. Figure (M-8-73). 1973. Canvas collage, 83.5 × 96.5 cm.

140

141. Figure (L-8-74). 1974. Canvas collage, 125.5 × 134.5 cm.

141

142. Drawing.

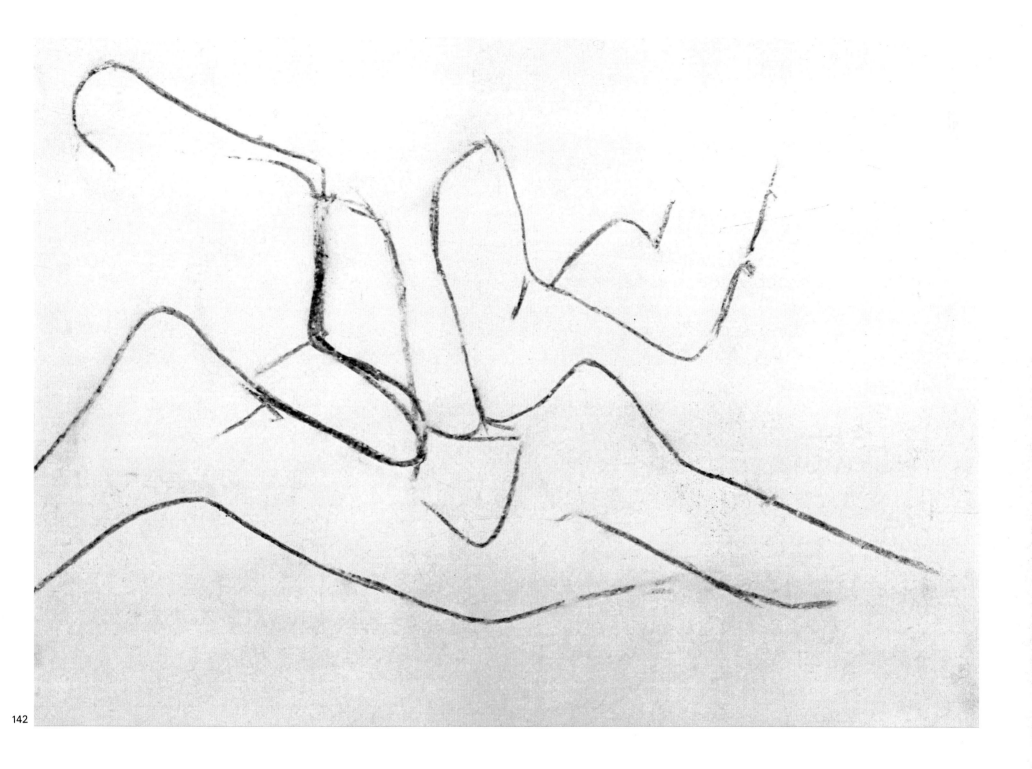

143. M-4-73. 1973. Canvas collage, 100 × 158.5 cm.

143

144. L-7-74. 1974. Newspaper collage, 132 × 182.5 cm.

144

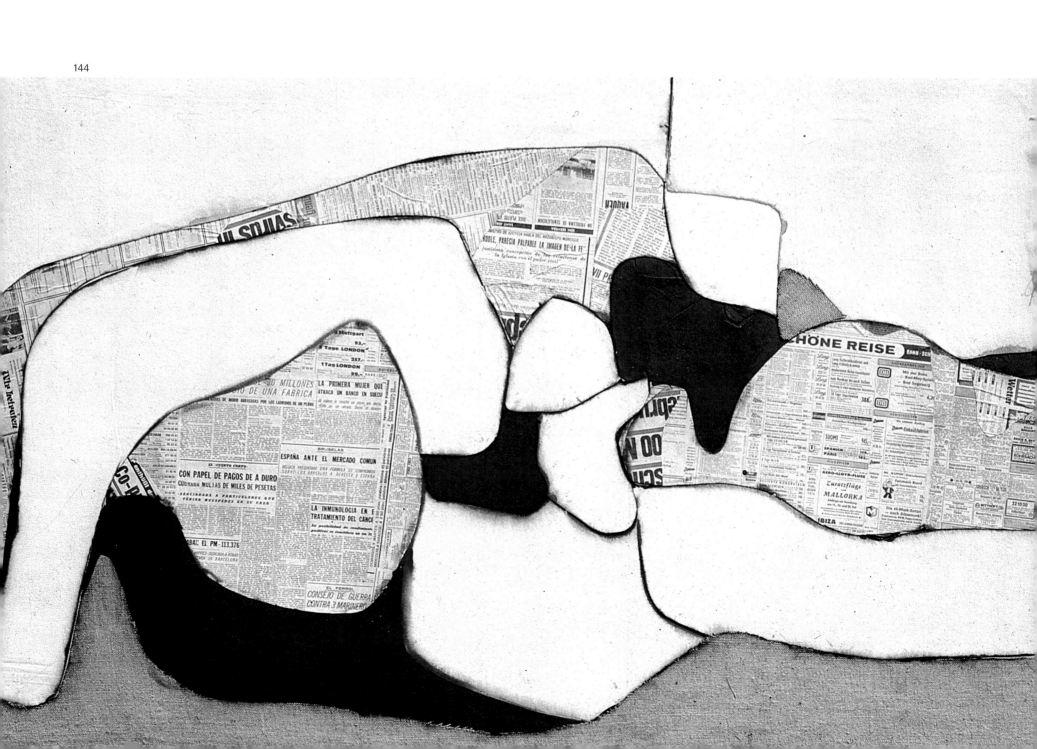

145. L-7-73. 1973. Canvas collage, 122 × 165 cm. Joaquín Bertrán Collection.

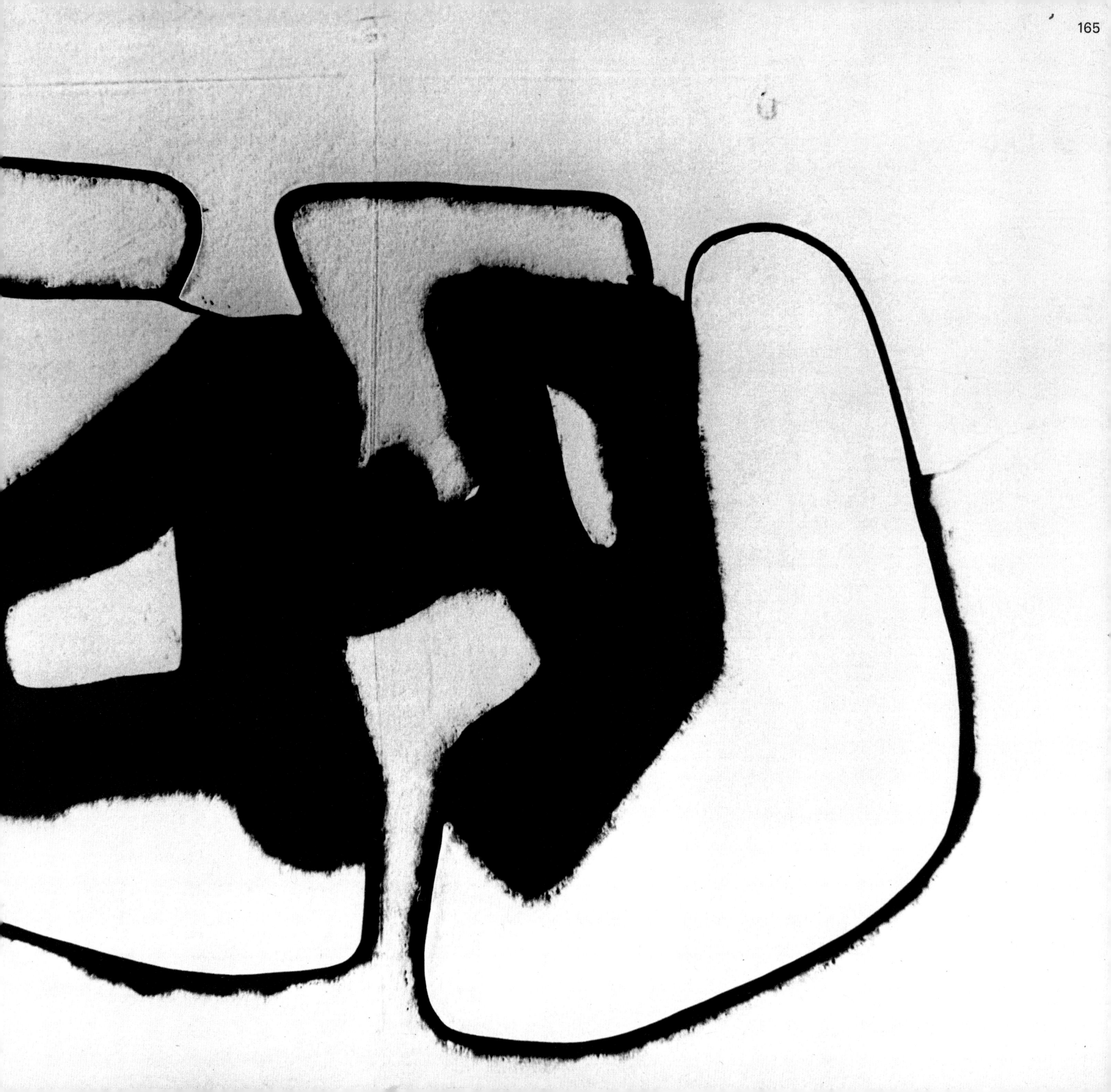

146. L-2-71. 1971. Canvas collage, 175 × 144 cm.

147. S-1-73. 1973. Canvas and newspaper collage, 53 × 65 cm.

148. S-1-72. 1972. Canvas collage, 59 × 64 cm.
149. M-2-73. 1973. Canvas and newspaper collage, 99 × 159 cm.

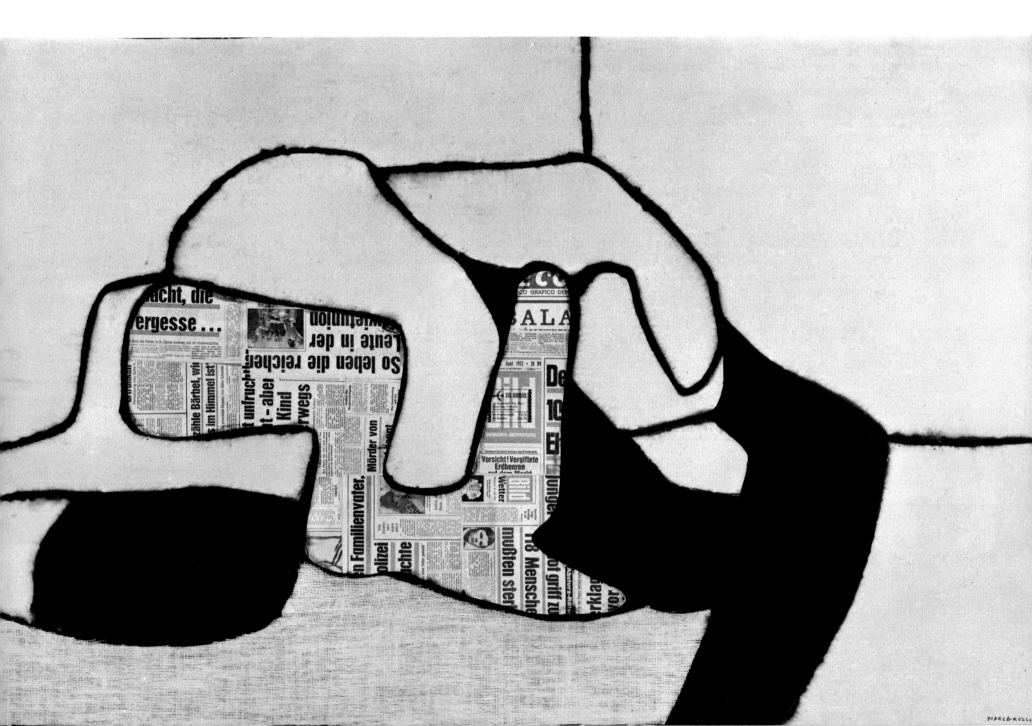

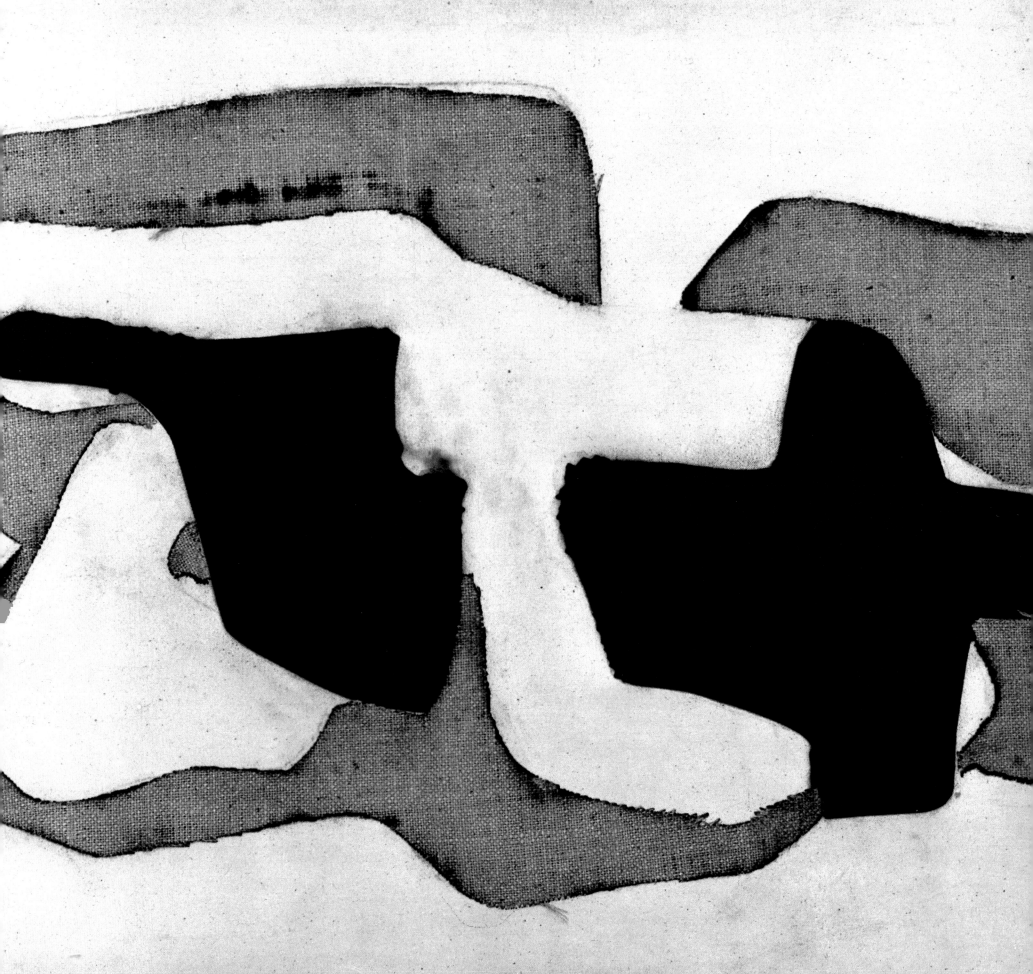

150. S-4-73. 1973. Canvas and newspaper collage, 53 × 65 cm.

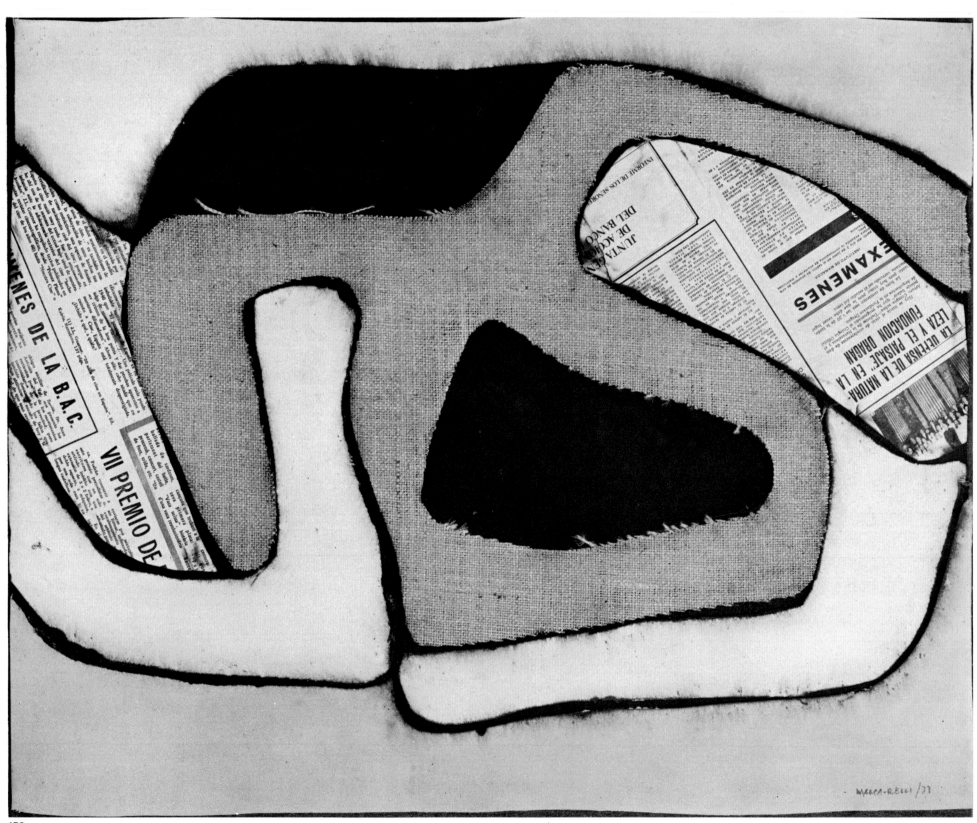

151. L-3-74. 1974. Oil and canvas collage, 132 × 182.8 cm.

152. Drawing.

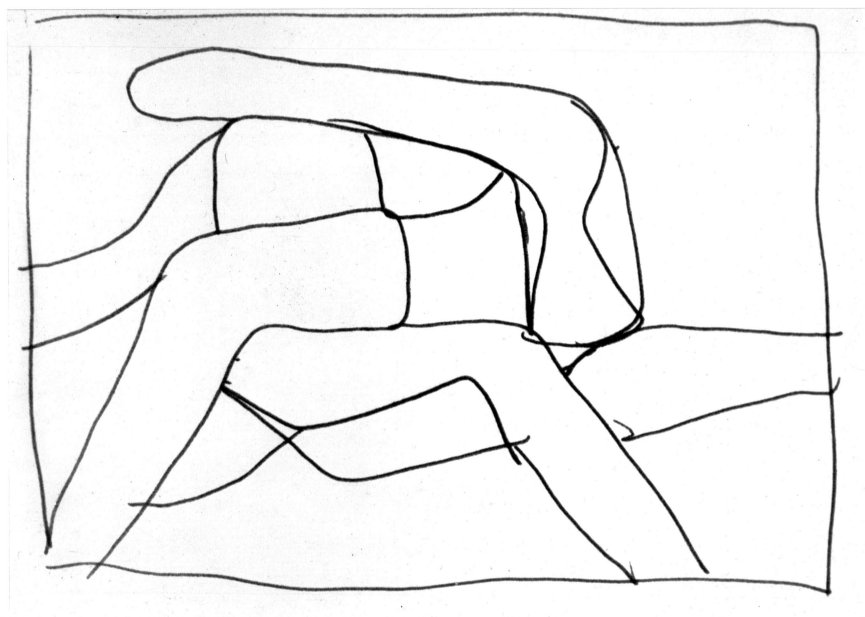

152

153. L-6-74. 1974. Oil and canvas collage, 144.8 × 182.8 cm.

153

154. L-12-74. 1974. Oil and canvas collage, 152.4 × 162.6 cm.
155. L-2-73. 1973. Oil and canvas collage, 149.9 × 170.2 cm.

156. Figure (S-5-74). 1974. Collage, 50 × 66 cm.

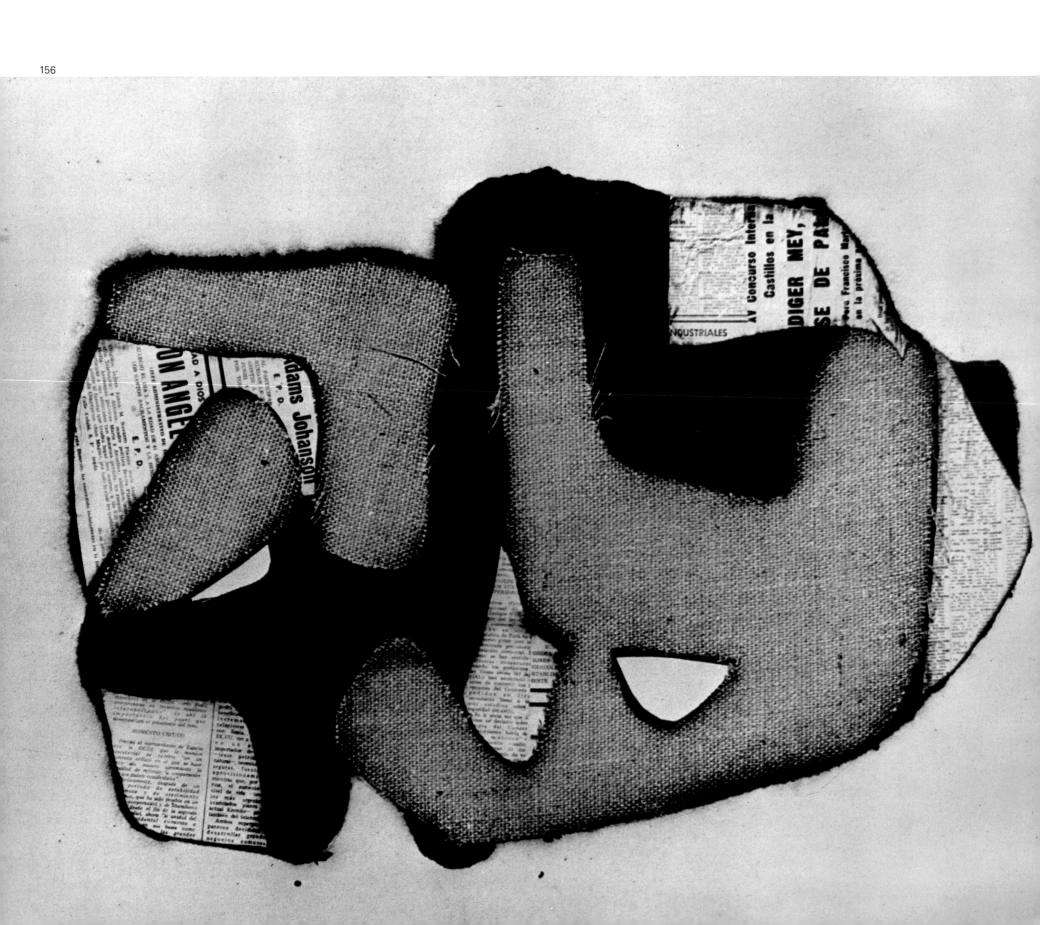

157. Figure (S-6-74). 1974. Collage, 66 × 50 cm.

158. M-11-73. 1973. Canvas collage, 85 × 95 cm.

159. L-11-74. 1974. Oil and canvas collage, 152.4 × 162.6 cm.

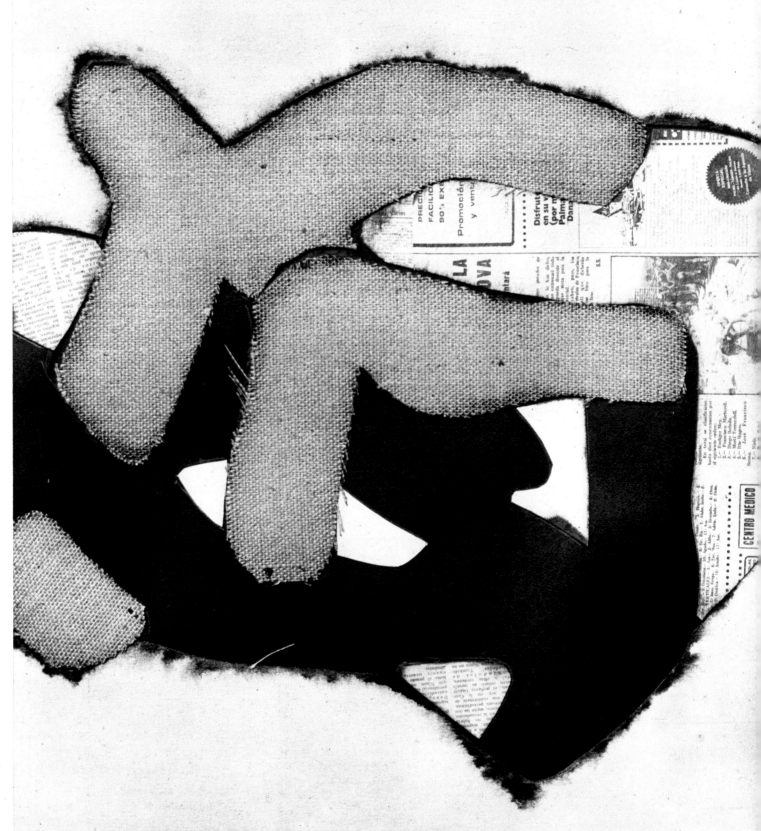

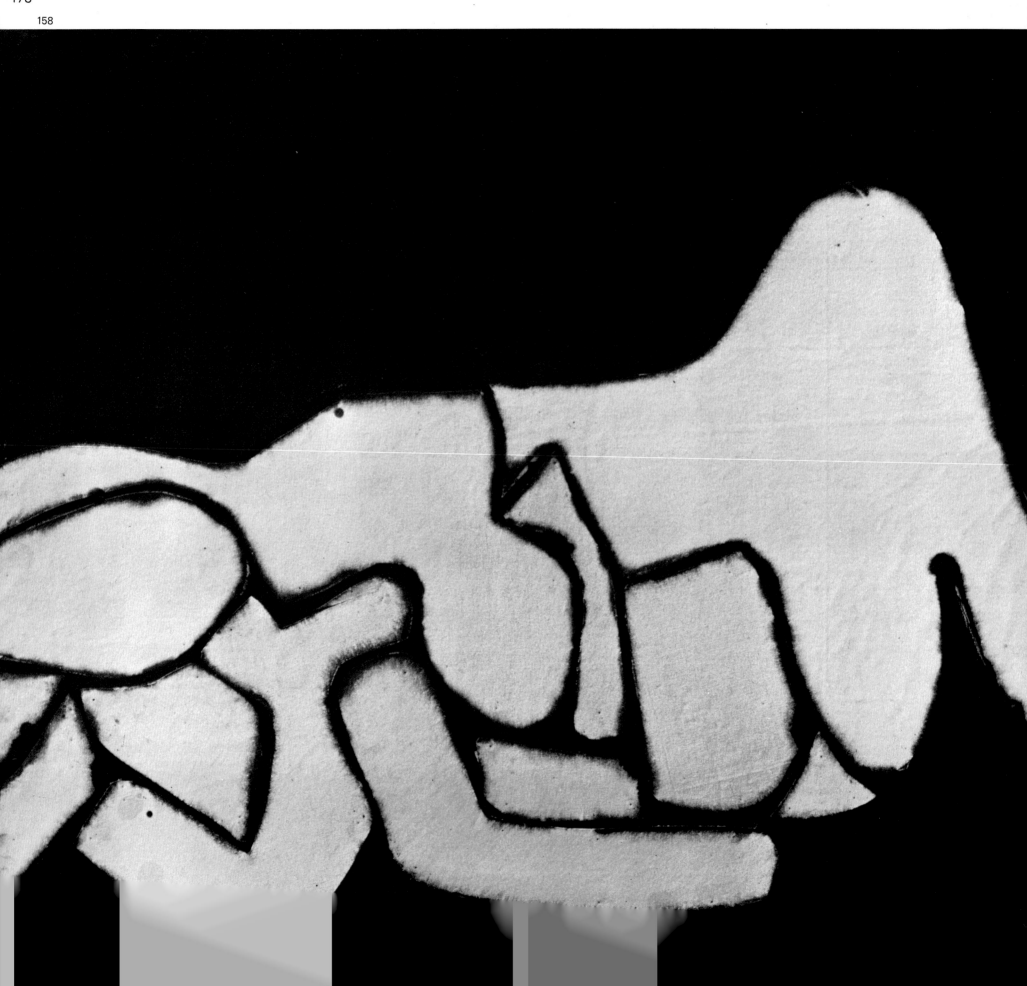

160. Figure (L-5-74). 1974. Canvas collage, 129.5 × 167.5 cm.
161. L-13-74. 1974. Oil and canvas collage, 149.9 × 162.6 cm.
162. The Wheel (L-15-74). 1974. Canvas collage, 152 × 152 cm.

163. Figure (L-9-73). 1973. Canvas collage, 139 × 176 cm.

163

164. L-16-74. 1974. Painted canvas collage, 137 × 177.5 cm.

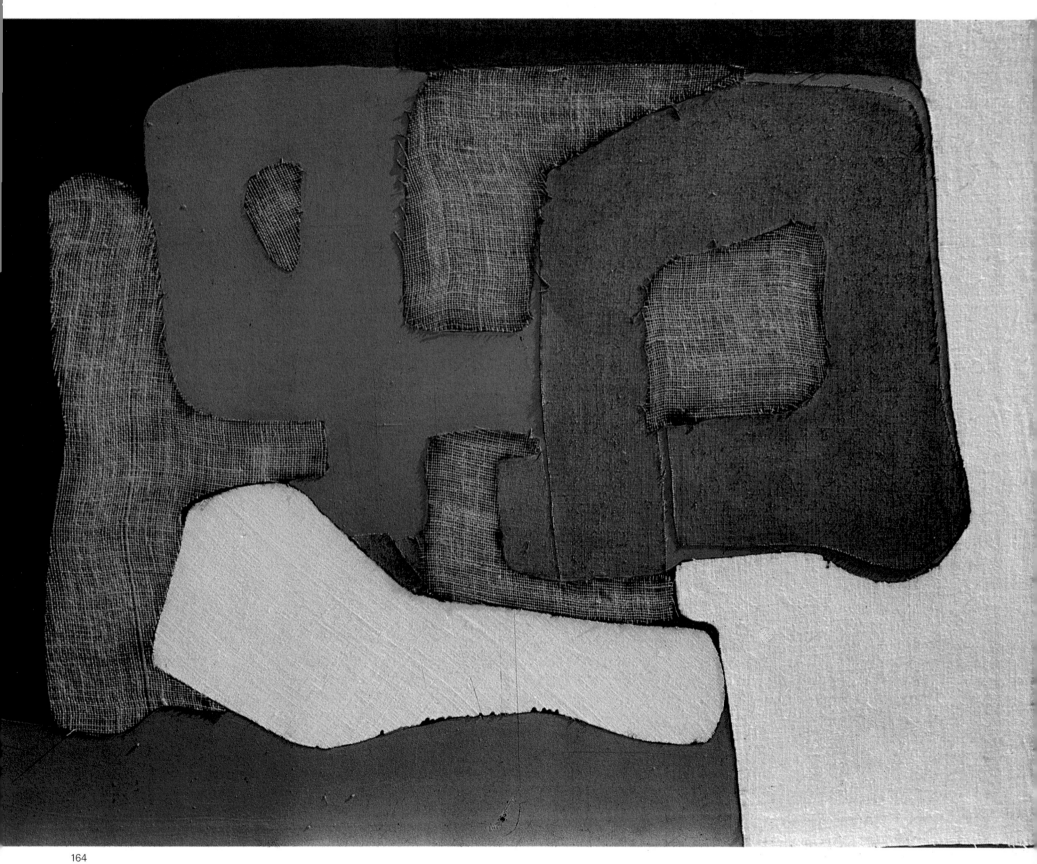

165. L-9-74. 1974. Canvas collage, 152.4 × 182.9 cm.

165

166.   L-14-74. 1974. Oil and canvas collage, 132 × 183 cm.

167. Figure (M-7-73). 1973. Canvas collage, 83.5 × 111.5 cm.

168. M-1-75. 1975. Canvas collage, 118 × 105 cm.

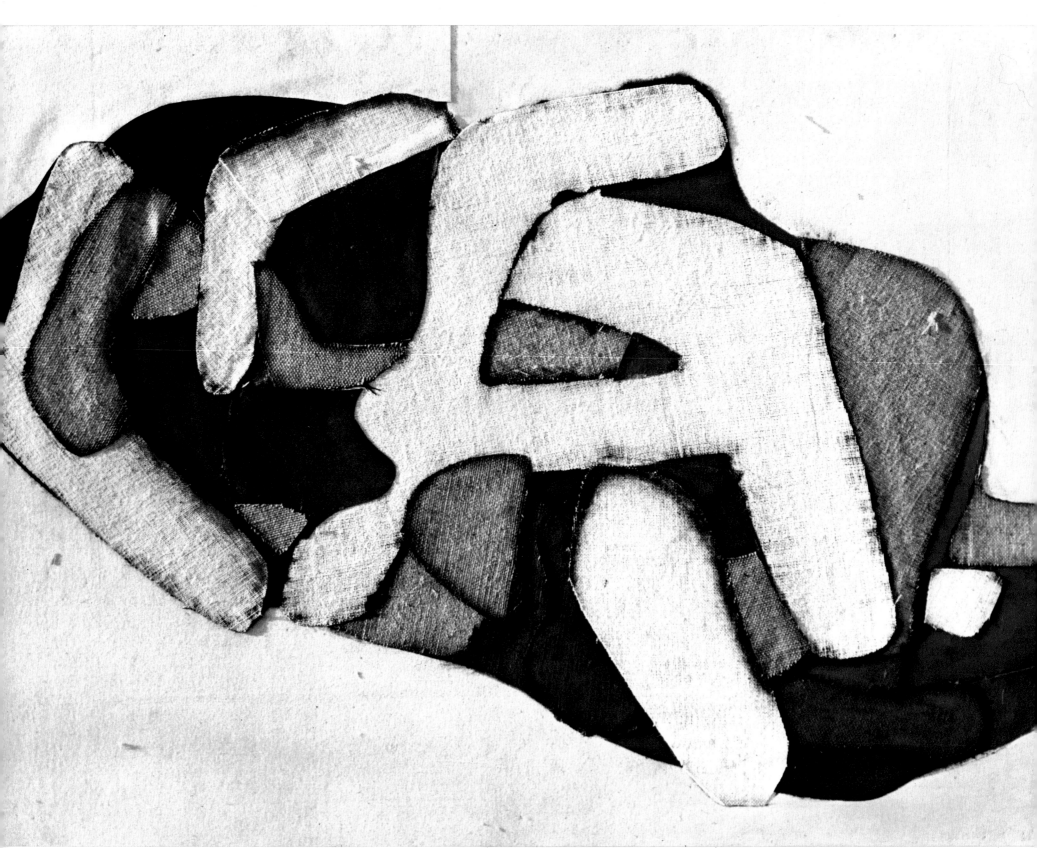

169. L-3-75. 1975. Canvas collage, 129.5 × 182.9 cm.

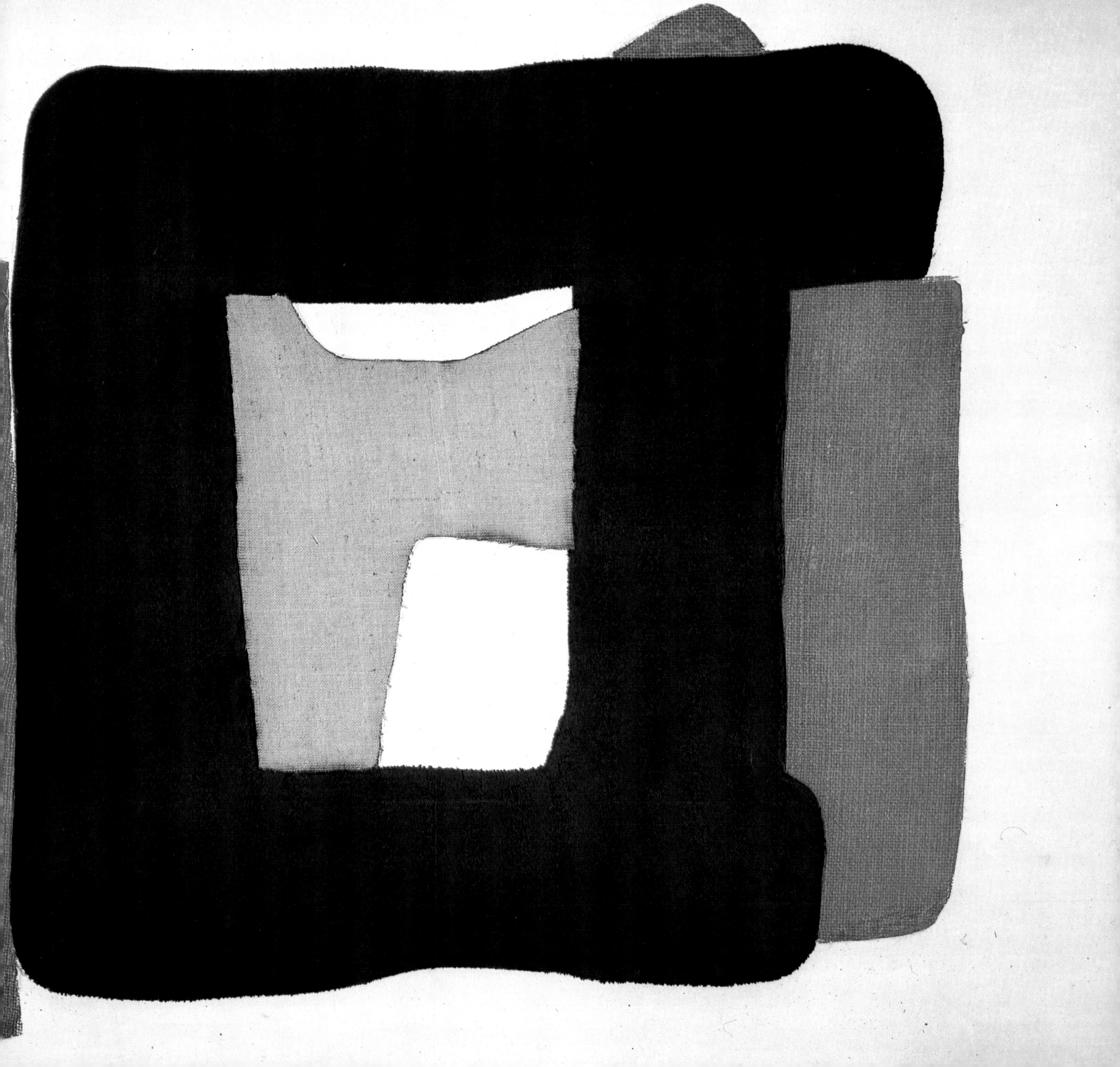

170. Figure (L-1-75). 1975. Canvas collage, 130 × 168 cm.

171. Figure (M-6-75). 1975. Canvas collage, 104 × 116 cm.

172. Figure (M-7-75). 1975. Newspaper and canvas collage, 104 × 116 cm.

173. Figure (M-4-75). 1975. Canvas collage, 104 × 116 cm.

170

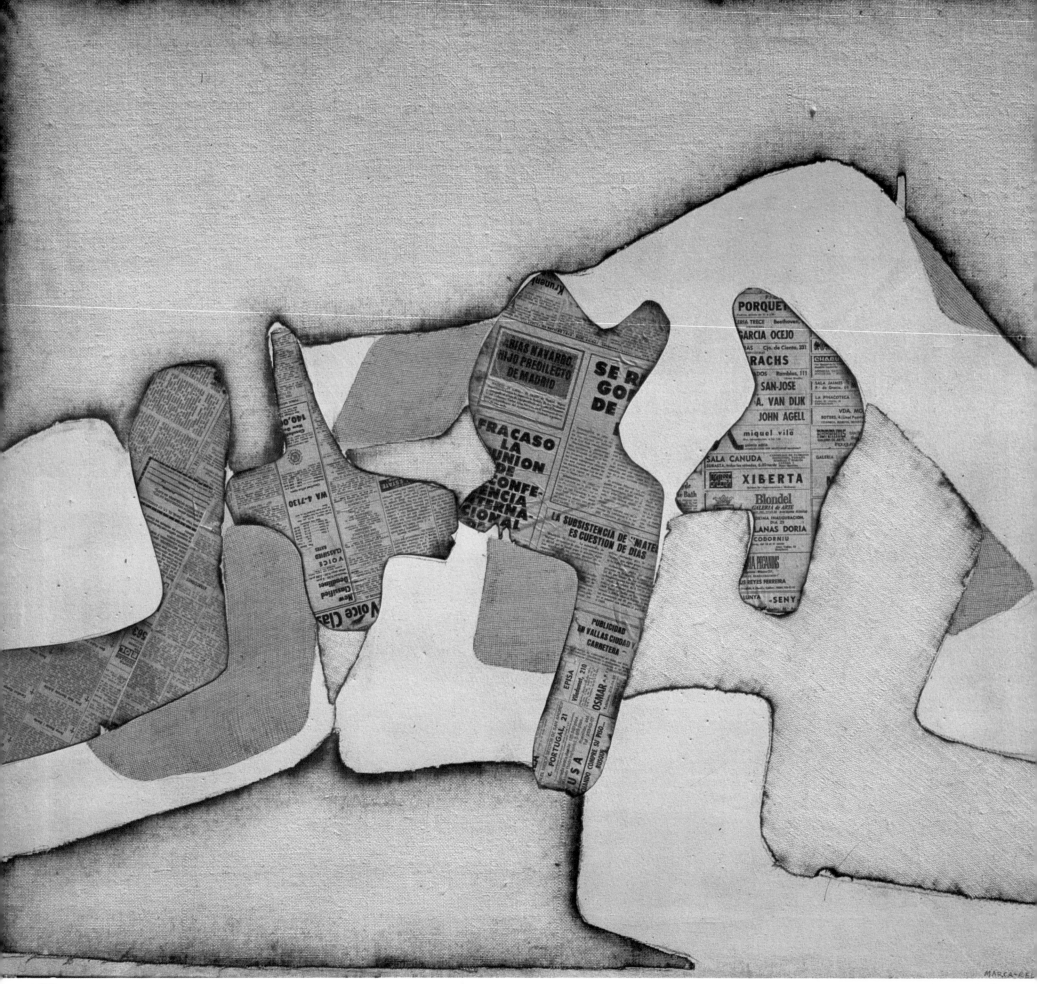

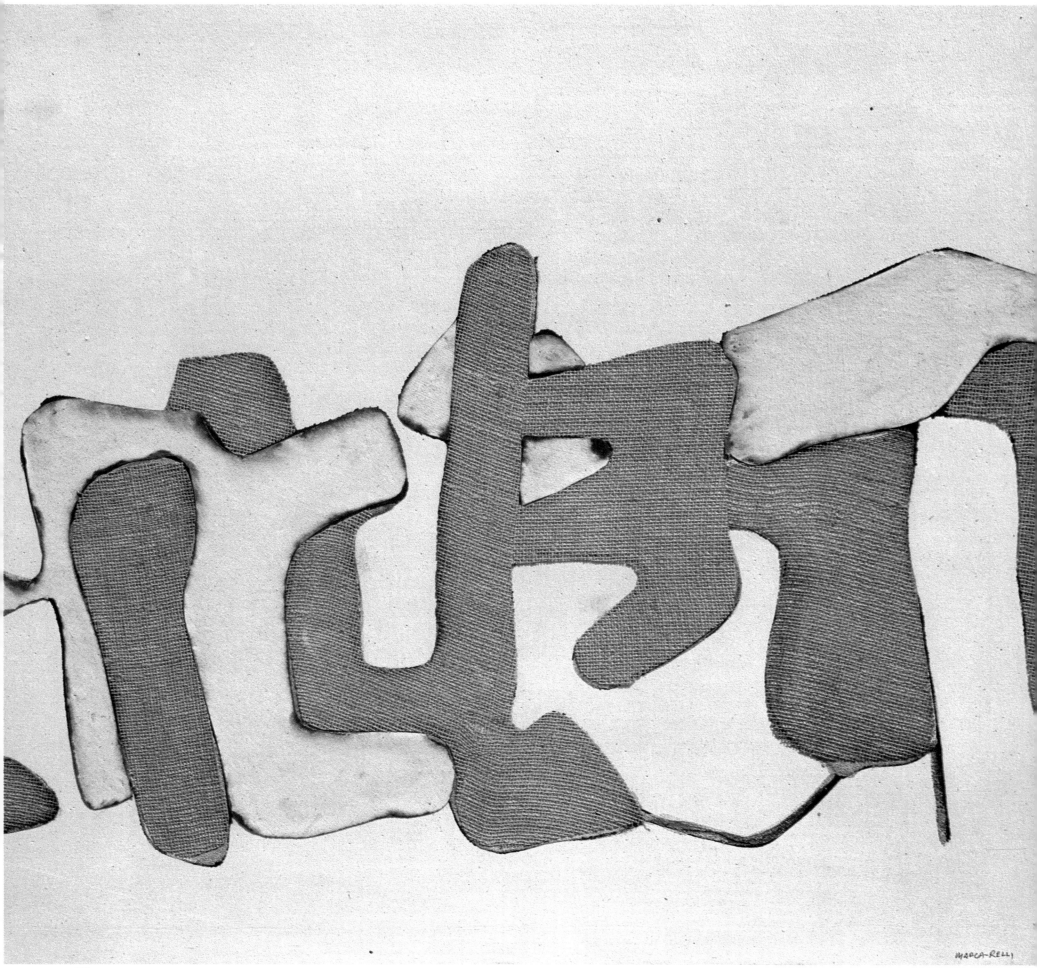

174

174. Drawing.
175. M-5-75. 1975. Newspaper and canvas collage, 94 × 116 cm.
176. Figure (M-20-75) 1975. Canvas collage, 104 × 114.2 cm.

177. Figure (M-19-75) 1975. Canvas collage, 104 × 116.8 cm.
178. M-8-75. 1975. Canvas collage, 106.6 × 116.8 cm.
179. M-18-75. 1975. Canvas collage, 106.6 × 116.8 cm.

175

179

CONRAD MARCA-RELLI

1, 2 & 3. *Conrad Marca-Relli in his Long Island studio, 1954.*

4. *House-cum-studio, adapted from a coach-house in East Hampton, Long Island, 1960-1969.*

5. *Conrad Marca-Relli and his wife, Anita Gibson, on board the Queen Elizabeth in 1956.*

1913.	Born in Boston on June 5th. First years of his life spent between Europe and Boston.
1926.	Family settles in New York.
1930.	Attends art classes. Begins to paint.
1935-1938.	Benefits from the WPA Federal Art Project (American Government aid programme for artists).
1940.	Visits Mexico.
1941-1945.	Military service during World War II.
1946.	Paints in New York.
1947.	First one-man show (Niveau Gallery, New York).
1948-1949.	Lives and works in Rome and Paris.
1949.	Returns to New York. With other painters founds the Eighth Street Club and takes an active part in organizing the First Artists Annual Show on Ninth Street.
1951.	Visits Rome again.
1952.	Returns to New York. Visits Mexico again. Settles in East Hampton, Long Island.
1954.	Is awarded the Logan Medal (First Prize of the Art Institute of Chicago). Visiting critic at Yale University.
1957.	Lives in Rome. Shows in Rome and Milan.
1958.	Visiting professor at the University of California, Berkeley.
1959.	Visiting critic at Yale University. Ford Fellowship.
1960.	First Purchase of the Detroit Institute of Arts.
1963.	M. U. Kohnstamm Prize of the Art Institute of Chicago.
1966.	Contract with the Marlborough-Gerson Gallery Inc., of New York. Resident artist at the New Collage of Sarasota, Florida.
1967.	Retrospective show at the Whitney Museum of American Art, New York.
1969-1972.	Lives and works in East Hampton, Long Island and in Sarasota, Florida.
1970-1975.	Also lives and works in Ibiza, Spain.
1976.	Elected member Institute of Arts & Letters.

6

7

PERSONAL EXHIBITIONS

1947.	Niveau Gallery, New York.
1949.	Galleria Il Cortile, Rome.
	Niveau Gallery, New York.
1951.	New Gallery, New York.
1953.	Stable Gallery, New York.
1955.	Stable Gallery, New York.
1956.	Stable Gallery, New York.
	Frank Perls Gallery, Hollywood.
1957.	Galleria la Tartaruga, Rome.
	Galleria del Naviglio, Milan.
1958.	Stable Gallery, New York.
1959.	Kootz Gallery, New York.
1960.	Kootz Gallery, New York.
	Playhouse Gallery, Sharon, Connecticut.
1961.	Kootz Gallery, New York.
	Bolles Gallery, San Francisco.
	Instituto de Arte Contemporáneo, Lima, Peru.
	Joan Peterson Gallery, Boston.
	Galerie Schmela, Düsseldorf (with Robert Motherwell).

6. *Conrad Marca-Relli working in his studio in Rome, 1956.*

7. *Exhibition at the Kootz Gallery, New York, 1964.*

8 & 9. *Exhibition in the University of Alabama, 1968.*

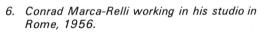

9

10

11

10, 11 & 12. Exhibition at the Marlborough Gallery, New York, 1970.

1962.	Kootz Gallery, New York. Galerie de France, Paris.	1970.	Marlborough Gallery, New York. University of Maryland Art Gallery, College Park, Maryland. Norton Gallery, West Palm Beach, Florida.
1963.	Galerie Charles Lienhard, Zurich. Kootz Gallery, New York. Tokyo Gallery, Tokyo.	1971.	Fort Lauderdale Museum of the Arts, Florida. Lowe Art Museum, University of Miami, Coral Gables, Florida. Galerie Schmela, Düsseldorf.
1964.	Kootz Gallery, New York.	1972.	Galería Carl Van der Voort, Ibiza, Spain.
1965.	Galeria Bonino, Buenos Aires.	1973.	Galería Inguanzo, Madrid. Galerie Numaga, Auvernier (Neuchatel), Switzerland.
1967.	James David Gallery, Coral Gables, Florida. Makler Gallery, Philadelphia. "Retrospective Exhibition", Whitney Museum of American Art, New York.	1974.	Marlborough Galerie, Zurich. Makler Gallery, Philadelphia.
1967-1968.	Rose Art Museum, Brandeis University, Waltham, Massachusetts.	1975.	Marlborough Gallery Inc., New York. Galería Carl Van der Voort, Ibiza, Spain. Marlborough-Goddard Gallery, Toronto and Montreal.
1968.	University of Alabama, Tuscaloosa. Alpha Gallery, Boston. Albright-Knox Members Gallery, Buffalo, New York.		
1969.	Reed College, Portland, Oregon. Seattle Art Museum, Seattle, Washington.		

13. *Exhibition at the Galería Carl Van der Voort, Ibiza, 1972.*

14, 15 & 16. *Exhibition at the Marlborough Galerie A.G., Zurich, 1974.*

1941.	"Soldier-Artists", Contemporary Art, New York.
1950.	"Abstraction Today", New Gallery, New York.
1953.	Whitney Museum of American Art Annual, New York (and in 1955-1957, 1959, 1961, 1963-1966 and 1969).
1954.	Art Institute of Chicago Annual (and in 1961 and 1963).
1955.	"XXVIII Biennale Internazionale d'Arte", Venice.
	"Pittsburgh International Exhibition", Carnegie Institute (and in 1958, 1961, 1964 and 1968).
1958.	"American Art", Brussels International Exhibition.
	Pennsylvania Academy of Fine Arts Annual (and in 1960, 1962 and 1965).
1959.	"American National Exhibition", Moscow.
	"Documental II", Kassel, Germany, organized by the Museum of Modern Art, New York.
	"V Bienal Estados Unidos", Museu de Arte Moderno, São Paulo.
1960.	Segunda Bienal Interamericana de México, Mexico.
	"Paths of Abstract Art", Cleveland Museum of Art.
	"60 American Painters", Walker Art Center, Minneapolis.
1961.	"The Art of Assemblage", The Museum of Modern Art, New York.
1962.	"Art Since 1950", Seattle World Fair.

1964.	"Between the Fairs", Whitney Museum of American Art, New York.
1965.	"The Twenty-Ninth Biennial Exhibition of Contemporary American Art", Corcoran Gallery of Art, Washington, D. C.
1966.	"Art of the United States", Whitney Museum of American Art, New York.
1967.	"White House Rotating Exhibition", organized by the Smithsonian Institution, Washington, D.C.
	"Art in Process: The Visual Development of a Collage", organized by The American Federation of Art, New York.
1968.	"Dorazio, Marca-Relli, Pasmore", Arts and Crafts Center, Pittsburgh. "International Sculpture", Galleria d'Arte Marlborough, Rome.
1968-1969.	"American Painting: the 1950's", travelling exhibition organized by the American Federation of Arts, New York.
1969-1970.	"American Drawings of the Sixties", New School Art Center, New York.
1970.	"Trends in Twentieth-Century Art", Art Gallery of the University of California, Santa Barbara, California.
	"II Bienal de Arte Coltejer", Medellín, Colombia.
	"American Painting 1970", Virginia Museum, Richmond, Virginia.

17

18

19

20

17, 18, 19 & 20.   Views of the house and studio in Ibiza.

21.   Posters for the different European exhibitions.

Albright-Knox Art Gallery, Buffalo, New York.
Art Institute of Chicago, Illinois.
Brandeis University, Waltham, Massachusetts.
Brundy Art Gallery, Waitsfield, Vermont.
Carnegie Institute, Pittsburgh, Pennsylvania.
Cleveland Museum of Art, Ohio.
Colby College Art Museum, Waterville, Maine.
Detroit Institute of Arts, Michigan.
Fogg Art Museum, Harvard University, Cambridge, Massachusetts.
Solomon R. Guggenheim Museum, New York.
Herron Museum of Art, Indianapolis, Indiana.
High Museum of Art, Atlanta, Georgia.
Houston Museum of Fine Art, Texas.
Los Angeles County Museum, California.
Memorial Art Gallery, Rochester, New York.
Metropolitan Museum of Art, New York.
James A. Michener Foundation, Allentown, Pennsylvania.

Minneapolis Institute of Arts, Minnesota.
Munson-Williams-Proctor Institute, Utica, New York.
Museum of Modern Art, New York.
Pennsylvania Academy of Fine Art, Philadelphia.
St. Paul Gallery of Art, Minnesota.
San Francisco Museum of Art, California.
Seattle Art Museum, Washington.
Wadsworth Atheneum, Hartford, Connecticut.
Walker Art Center, Minneapolis, Minnesota.
Washington University, St. Louis, Missouri.
Whitney Museum of American Art, New York.
University of Alabama, Tuscaloosa.
University of Michigan, Ann Arbor.
University of Nebraska Art Galleries, Lincoln.
Yale University, New Haven, Connecticut.
Museo de Arte Contemporáneo, Ibiza.

21

22. *Illustration in* Time *Magazine, from a report on the picture* The Battle *in the Metropolitan Museum, New York.*

23, 24, 25 & 26. *Different views of the retrospective exhibition presented by the Whitney Museum of American Art, New York, in 1967.*

22

24

23

25

VILLA, EMILIO: *Arte Visiva,* Roma, 1955.

PERILLI, ACHILLER: *Civiltà di Macchine,* 1958.

TYLER, PARKER: *Marca-Relli,* "The Pocket Museum", Editions Georges Fall, Paris, 1960.

ARNASON, H. H.: *Marca-Relli,* Harry N. Abrams, Inc., New York, 1961.

AGEE, WILLIAM C.: *Marca-Relli,* Whitney Museum of American Art, New York, 1967.

ARNASON, H. H.: *60 American Painters,* Abstract Expressionist Painting of the Fifties. Walker Art Center, Minneapolis, Minnesota, 1960.

HENNING, EDWARD B.: *Paths of Abstract Art,* The Cleveland Museum of Art, Harry N. Abrams, Inc., New York, 1960.

ARNASON, H. H. and GUGGENHEIM, HARRY F.: *American Abstract,* Expressionists and Imagists, The Solomon R. Guggenheim Museum, New York, 1961.

Art USA Now. Catalogue, 1961.

BARR, RANDOLPH. *Art USA Now,* Lee Nordness (vol. II). C. J. Bucher Ltd., Lucerne, 1962.

SPEYER, A. JAMES: *66th American Exhibition,* Directions in Contemporary Painting and Sculpture, The Art Institute of Chicago, 1963.

NIZON, PAUL: *Conrad Marca-Relli,* Galerie Charles Lienhard, Zurich, 1963.

HUNTER, SAM: *New Directions in American Painting,* The Poses Institute of Fine Arts, Brandeis University, Waltham, Massachussetts, 1963.

URIBE, BASILIO: *Marca-Relli,* Galería Bonino, Buenos Aires, 1965.

SEITZ, WILLIAM: *Brandeis University,* Waltham, Massachusetts, 1967.

SELZ, NORA, et al.: *Selection 1967: Recent Acquisitions in Modern Art,* University of California, Berkeley, 1967.

TAPIÉ, MICHEL:*L'aventure informelle,* Gutaî, 8 - Tokyo, Japan, 1967.

SWEENEY, JAMES JOHNSON: *Signals in the 'Sixties',* Honolulu Academy of Arts, 1968.

LEIRIS, ALAIN DE: *Marca-Relli: Collage and Gottlieb: Sculpture,* University of Maryland Art Gallery, 1970.

AYLLON, JOSÉ: *Marca-Relli,* Galería Inguanzo, Madrid, 1972.

INDEX OF WORKS

67. Sculpture 1 (S-C-P-1). 1969. Marble and slate, 37 × 37 × 2 cm. Private collection.

68. U-4. 1966. Aluminium sculpture, 122 × 142 × 17 cm.

69. XS-1-67. 1967. Canvas collage, 61 × 61 cm. Alfred Schmela Collection, Düsseldorf.

70. L-2-66. 1966. Canvas collage, 183 × 152.5 cm. Private collection.

71. QM-1-66. 1966. Canvas collage, 96.5 × 114 cm. Private collection.

72. Drawing.

73. F-M-6-67. 1967. Painted canvas collage, 81 × 91.5 cm.

74. F-M-9-67. 1967. Painted canvas collage, 81 × 91.7 cm.

75. L-16-69. 1969. Canvas collage, 155 × 167.5 cm.

76. F-M-10-67. 1967. Painted canvas collage, 81 × 91.5 cm.

77. Untitled. 1963. Canvas and wax collage, 28.5 × 40.5 cm.

78. Image 4 (L-4-69). 1969. Mixed media collage on canvas, 176.5 × 145 cm.

79. Image 18 (L-18-68-69). 1969-1970. Mixed media collage on canvas, 152 × 183 cm. Private collection.

80. Untitled relief 1. 1969. Plexiglass. 39.5 × 65 cm.

81. Untitled relief 2. 1969. Plexiglass and wood, 38 × 63.5 cm.

82. L-2-72. 1972. Canvas collage, 176.5 × 144.5 cm.

83. L-21-69. 1969. Canvas collage, 147.3 × 181.6 cm.

84. Sculpture 2 (S-C-P-2). Marble and slate, 35 × 13 × 2 cm.

85. Drawing.

86. L-1-72. 1972. Canvas collage, 155.5 × 175.8 cm.

87. L-4-72. 1972. Canvas collage, 155.5 × 175.8 cm. Private collection.

88. L-3-72. Canvas collage, 156 × 171 cm.

89. Drawing.

90. L-70. 1970. Canvas collage, 157 × 192 cm. Galerie Schmela Collection, Düsseldorf.

91. Drawing.

92. I-L-6-72. 1972. Canvas collage, 153 × 168 cm.

93. LL-2-72-A & B. B & C. 1972. Canvas collage, 240 × 164 cm.

94. M-9-71. 1971. Oil and canvas collage, 81.3 × 91.5 cm.

95. S-6-73. 1973. Canvas collage, 50 × 65 cm.

96. Drawing.

97. M-12-71. 1971. Canvas collage, 91.5 × 81 cm.

98. Figure (S-3-65). 1965. Canvas collage, 55.5 × 48 cm.

99. Reclining Figure (X5-20-68). 1969. Painted canvas collage, 55.5 × 61 cm.

100. Figure (Y-M-8-70). 1970. Collage, 63.5 × 86 cm.

101. L-1-71. 1971. Painted canvas collage, 167.5 × 167.5 cm.

102. XM-20-71. 1971. Canvas collage, 81 × 91.5 cm.

103. Drawing.

104. Drawing.

105. L-5-66. 1966. Canvas collage, 122 × 167.5 cm.

106. Multiple image (L-14-69). 1969. Mixed media collage on canvas, 145 × 176.5 cm.

107. Untitled (S-1-69). 1969. Canvas collage, 61 × 56 cm.

108. Figure-Form I (M-1-66). 1966. Painted canvas collage, 89 × 114 cm.

109. Drawing.

110. Drawing.

111. Torso (L-1-69). 1969. Mixed media collage on canvas, 145.5 × 176.5 cm. Private collection.

112. Reclining figure (F-L-6-67). 1967. Painted canvas collage, 144.5 × 176.5 cm.

113. Drawing.

114. M-3-72. 1972. Canvas collage, 81 × 86 cm.

115. M-11-71. 1971. Oil and canvas collage, 32 × 36 cm.

116. Figure (X-L-2-70-71). 1970-1971. Canvas collage, 177 × 144 cm.

117. X-M-4-70. 1970. Canvas collage, 81 × 91.5 cm.

118. X-M-7-70. 1970. Canvas collage, 81 × 91.5 cm.

119. M-6-71. 1971. Canvas collage, 81 × 91.5 cm.

120. Untitled relief No. 6 (R-SCP-6-69). 1969. Mixed media, 56 × 36 cm.

121. M-12-71. 1971. Canvas collage, 81 × 91.5 cm.

122. LL-2-71. A & B. 1971. Painted canvas collage, 228 × 168 cm.

123. M-8-71. 1971. Canvas collage, 81 × 91.5 cm.

124. M-10-71. 1971. Canvas collage, 81 × 91.5 cm.

125. Drawing.

126. S-3-73. 1973. Newspaper collage, 53 × 65 cm.

127. Cupsy (S-15-72). 1972. Newspaper collage, 52 × 65 cm.

128. Figure (S-9-73). 1973. Newspaper collage, 66 × 50 cm.

129. Drawing.

130. Figure (OS-20-73). 1973. Collage, 53 × 71 cm.

131. Figures (M-14-71). 1971. Canvas collage, 81.3 × 122 cm.

132. Drawing.

133. M-1-73. 1973. Canvas and newspaper collage, 99 × 159 cm.

134. Y-M-15-71. 1971. Canvas collage, 81.3 × 175.8 cm.

135. Figure (M-9-73). 1973. Canvas collage, 94 × 116 cm.

136. Drawing.

137. M-3-73. 1973. Canvas and newspaper collage, 99 × 159 cm.

138. S-4-72. 1972. Newspaper collage, 51 × 65 cm. Private collection.

139. S-2-73. 1973. Canvas collage, 99 × 159 cm.

140. Figure (M-8-73). 1973. Canvas collage, 83.5 × 96.5 cm.

141. Figure (L-8-74). 1974. Canvas collage, 125.5 × 134.5 cm.

142. Drawing.

143. M-4-73. 1973. Canvas collage, 100 × 158.5 cm.

144. L-7-74. 1974. Newspaper collage, 132 × 182.5 cm.

145. L-7-73. 1973. Canvas collage, 122 × 165 cm. Joaquín Bertrán Collection.

146. L-2-71. 1971. Canvas collage, 175 × 144 cm.

147. S-1-73. 1973. Canvas and newspaper collage, 53 × 65 cm.

148. S-1-72. 1972. Canvas collage, 59 × 64 cm.

149. M-2-73. 1973. Canvas and newspaper collage, 99 × 159 cm.

150. S-4-73. 1973. Canvas and newspaper collage, 53 × 65 cm.

151. L-3-74. 1974. Oil and canvas collage, 132 × 182.8 cm.

152. Drawing.

153. L-6-74. 1974. Oil and canvas collage, 144.8 × 182.8 cm.

154. L-12-74. 1974. Oil and canvas collage, 152.4 × 162.6 cm.

155. L-2-73. 1973. Oil and canvas collage, 149.9 × 170.2 cm.

156. Figure (S-5-74). 1974. Collage, 50 × 66 cm.

157. Figure (S-6-74). 1974. Collage, 66 × 50 cm.

158. M-11-73. 1973. Canvas collage, 85 × 95 cm.

159. L-11-74. 1974. Oil and canvas collage, 152.4 × 162.6 cm.

160. Figure (L-5-74). 1974. Canvas collage, 129.5 × 167.5 cm.

161. L-13-74. 1974. Oil and canvas collage, 149.9 × 162.6 cm.

162. The Wheel (L-15-74). 1974. Canvas collage, 152 × 152 cm.

163. Figure (L-9-73). 1973. Canvas collage, 139 × 176 cm.

164. L-16-74. 1974. Painted canvas collage, 137 × 177.5 cm.

165. L-9-74. 1974. Canvas collage, 152.4 × 182.9 cm.

166. L-14-74. 1974. Oil and canvas collage, 132 × 183 cm.

167. Figure (M-7-73). 1973. Canvas collage, 83.5 × 111.5 cm.

168. M-1-75. 1975. Canvas collage, 118 × 105 cm.

169. L-3-75. 1975. Canvas collage, 129.5 × 182.9 cm.

170. Figure (L-1-75). 1975. Canvas collage, 130 × 168 cm.

171. Figure (M-6-75). 1975. Canvas collage, 104 × 116 cm.

172. Figure (M-7-75). 1975. Newspaper and canvas collage, 104 × 116 cm.

173. Figure (M-4-75). 1975. Canvas collage, 104 × 116 cm.
174. Drawing.

175. M-5-75. 1975. Newspaper and canvas collage, 94 × 116 cm.

176. Figure (M-20-75) 1975. Canvas collage, 104 × 114.2 cm.

177. Figure (M-19-75) 1975. Canvas collage, 104 × 116.8 cm.

178. M-8-75. 1975. Canvas collage, 106.6 × 116.8 cm.

179. M-18-75. 1975. Canvas collage, 106.6 × 116.8 cm.